Senior Living Investing Made Easy

Earn Excellent Returns While Providing a Better Life for Seniors

The sequel to the #1 International Best-Selling Books

"Apartment Syndication Made Easy"

and "Positivity Brings Profitability"

By Vinney (Smile) Chopra

Senior Living Investing Made Easy. - 1st ed.

ISBN: 9798861930390

Grab your Free Book Bonuses at:

www.VinneyChopra.com/FreeBenefits

Or Scan This Code:

www.VinneyChopra.com/FreeBenefits

Dedication

This book is dedicated to all the amazing people I've encountered over my career, including mentors, teachers, relatives, friends, and my mastermind and Inner Circle student investors, who continue to inspire me daily.

If wealth can be measured by the people who enrich our lives, then I am indeed a very rich man.

I would also like to dedicate this book to my wife, Kanchan, and our two wonderful children, Neil and Monica. You are all a source of love, memories, encouragement, and motivation, and you make my life complete.

Finally, this book might not have happened at all were it not for my grandfather and uncle, both of whom gave me the gift of opportunity by bringing me to the United States of America to pursue my dreams and become a better person. You are both the inspiration behind this work.

I have always believed and lived by this quote:

"I have always believed in an individual's

ability to shape the world around them through

positivity, enthusiasm, and massive selfless actions."

—Vinney (Smile) Chopra

"Happiness is when what you think, what you say, and what you do are
in harmony."

– Mahatma Gandhi

"If you want others to be happy, practice compassion.

If you want to be happy, practice compassion."

– Dalai Lama

"The greatest discovery of all time is that a person can change his
future
by merely changing his attitude."

– Oprah Winfrey

Table of Contents

Forward

I have known Vinney (Smile) Chopra since 2011, and I consider him both a valued client and one of my greatest friends. I met Vinney when he first came to my former corporate securities law firm looking for documents for his first multi-family syndication. In just eight years, he built a portfolio of approximately 4,000 multi-family units in 26 syndicated properties. He has subsequently created a network of Senior Living facilities that are dedicated to improving the lives of the senior residents, their families, and the caring staff members who attend them.

Vinney is the epitome of the American Dream. He came to the US as an immigrant with $7.00 in his pocket, believing that America was the land of plenty and that he could achieve any goal.

What is the American Dream? It's "the belief that anyone, regardless of where they were born or what class they were born into, can attain their own version of success in a society in which upward mobility is possible for everyone. The American dream is believed to be achieved through sacrifice, risk-taking, and hard work, rather than by chance." *Investopedia.com*

Through hard work, perseverance, and an undaunted spirit, Vinney is one of the few who have made the American Dream a reality.

When I counsel new syndication clients, especially those nervous about the legalities of raising private capital or structuring a syndicate, I ask if they know Vinney Chopra. If they don't, I tell them they should get to know him and then tell them his story.

Why? We all need to think a little more like Vinney. He came to this beautiful country believing anything was possible and forged ahead without letting fear or hesitation slow his steps. And he stayed open-minded and continued to absorb knowledge from other experts and mentors along the way.

The best thing about Vinney is his enthusiasm and gratitude for life. He shows it by giving back. At every opportunity, Vinney looks for ways to add value to the lives of others, whether they are his real estate coaching students, readers of his books, other syndicators, staff members, or residents in his properties. Vinney treats everyone he meets as if they are a valued addition to his inner circle.

Vinney lives each day with an abundance mindset, believing *everyone* can achieve their wildest dreams. Because he so willingly shares his journey to inspire others, the Universe seems to shower Vinney and those around him with good fortune.

We can all learn from Vinney – much more than how to buy real estate. As you read this book, accept Vinney's gift of knowledge about investing in residential assisted living with gratitude. Help him spread the word to others who need inspiration – and you, too, could soon see abundance touch your own life.

I am honored to have been able to edit this book for Vinney, for he has touched my life in many ways – and I know he can make a difference in your life too.

Kim Lisa Taylor, Esq.

Why I Wrote This Book

Providing For The Generation That Provided For Us

According to Statista.com, it is estimated that over a fifth (20 percent) of the population in the United States will be 65 years or older by 2050 (compared to only 15.6% today). If we consider the quality of living conditions that our seniors call "home," we will undoubtedly find them lacking—and given how many seniors will be and are currently among us, this is certainly cause for alarm.

With a rapidly aging population, we must start planning how we will house and care for the senior population in the future. In 2019, the not-for-profit Senior Living organization, National Senior Campuses, reported only 21,000 Senior Living units across the United States.

Other than housing, personal and medical care for seniors is another pressing issue with massive potential for growth in the coming years. Among the population of older adults in the United States, almost seven percent require personal care from other persons, often in the form of meal preparation, transportation, and help with personal grooming.

Our elderly are the people who connect us to our past. They are also, however, among our most vulnerable citizens. Safe and adequate housing accommodations should be an essential requirement for the well-being of all people. Yet, there needs to be more consideration given to accommodating the aging population or improving their quality of life.

What will we do as we move toward the last stages of life and end up in the same types of facilities that we are currently subjecting our senior citizens to? How will we cope? Should we wait until it is too late to make preparations for tomorrow? We all know that the aging population deserves better treatment and that investing in Senior Living is the right path for future generations.

Hi, this is Vinney Chopra, the author. You may be asking, why this book? I have been investing in Commercial and Residential real estate for over 40 years. I wrote a best-selling book, "Apartment Syndication Made Easy," that got rave reviews.

Since my life has been a total result of positivity and an abundance mindset, I wrote my second top seller, "Positivity Brings Profitability." I came to the USA with $7 and dreams of making an impact in this great land of opportunity.

As I turned 65+ myself, my focus shifted to Senior Living in the multifamily sector. I started researching and analyzing the demands and challenges of this sector. In a bid to make Senior Living communities available to senior citizens, *Moneil Senior Living* partnered with Build Senior Living in December 2019 to build affordable Senior Living projects that encourage an enriching lifestyle. Our focus has been to provide great quality housing and caring service to seniors in their golden years of life by designing, building, and managing Senior Living communities.

Now, I wish to share what I have learned with you, my devoted followers and readers. As we dive into this journey together, it is crucial to understand why I wrote this book and why I am more excited than ever to share this excellent asset class with you.

Things I Want You To Keep In Mind

Investing (particularly in the Senior Living sector) can seem complicated at first glance, which is why I embarked on my quest to make this book as easy to understand as possible. Keep in mind, however, that despite our hard work, this instruction ***was*** written by a seasoned investor who has performed years' worth of research on this topic and has been an active Senior Living investor for many years.

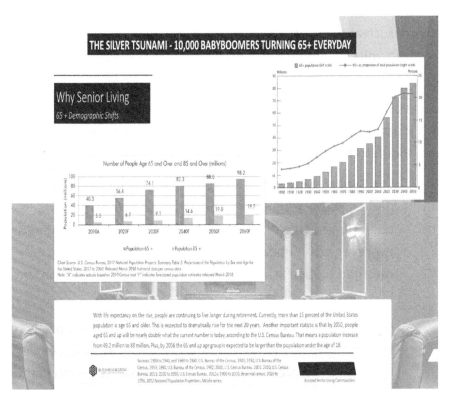

I have used the terms "Senior Living" and "senior housing" somewhat interchangeably throughout this book. They both essentially refer to places seniors live. However, there are many different levels of amenities and care involved in Senior Living based on resident lifestyle needs, desires, and affordability, all of which we will explore in this book.

The phrase "senior housing" tends to evoke a picture of an institutional facility, the traditional "rest home" or "nursing home" where seniors used to be left in others' care and often forgotten by their loved ones, or an apartment complex where seniors live in isolation. "Senior Living," on the other hand, is far more descriptive of the active and vibrant lifestyle we want our seniors to enjoy with comfortable surroundings, pleasant activities, social gatherings, and a sense of community – all of which we hope to enjoy someday too! So, where possible, throughout this book, I have used the phrase "Senior Living," often accompanied by a word such as property, facility, project, home, housing, establishment, or community, to describe this excellent and growing asset class.

My team and I have compiled a list of points that we believe are necessary for you to know before we get started so that we can begin this journey on the same page. As you read, here are the primary points you should keep in mind:

- The Senior Living sector indeed experienced both a steep decline in the number of occupants and a stark rise in operation-related expenses due to the COVID-19 pandemic. However, the number of new-resident move-ins has since returned to (and in some cases has even increased from) pre-COVID levels.

- Occupancy loss during the pandemic was attributed partly to stricter move-in criteria and slower processing times, which have since returned to normal with the release of vaccination protocols and better application processing procedures.

- This rapid bounce-back of demand, which has been far greater than nearly any other real estate asset class, accurately demonstrates the essential nature of the Senior Living industry.

- While the pandemic has disproportionately affected the elderly, the implications to residents were far more severe in skilled nursing sectors than in assisted living and memory care. For reference, the latter is what we will be focusing on as the investment opportunity in this book.

- Currently, the US is on track to have more seniors than young people by 2035. This is due to the generation known as "Baby Boomers" finally aging into retirement. Between 2020 and 2025, the 75 and up population is forecasted to increase by over 1 million annually and 48.1% over the course of the decade. This growth is more than three times what we've seen in the past decade.

- Because of the stark rise forecasted in the number of seniors, the continued demand for this sector is all but guaranteed to skyrocket in the coming years. That makes right now the time to learn about and invest in Senior Living facilities to acquire the greatest gains.

- The cost for typical in-home health options is 59% to 61% more expensive than assisted-living communities, making Senior Living homes the preferred elderly care solution.

- While seniors are living longer, they are doing so with a greater number of chronic conditions requiring personal care treatment, such as Alzheimer's, obesity, and diabetes. Because of this, having regular access to medical staff and care procedures is a must.

- Senior Living homes, where multiple seniors can live together, are considered a significant part of the solution to the immense volume and cost of caring for the elderly population.

Now, I encourage you to read those facts first to interpret them and then a second time to truly understand the impact they will have on your journey. In the world of investing, the best way to get ahead is to see real-world events and use those to predict the ups and downs in the industry in which you'd like to invest your money.

The statistics I've listed above should tell you that **now is the time to invest in Senior Living.** Not only is there predicted to be a stark increase in demand, but the sector has also demonstrated its resiliency in bouncing back from an international crisis.

Most investors spend their entire lives looking for the perfect sector to invest in—one that combines the lowest risk and highest reward. However, because of the volatile nature of most investment opportunities, they can never find that so-called "golden egg."

Luckily, you don't have to spend time on pointless pursuits like that. Instead, I've found it for you, and I'm laying this golden egg opportunity directly in your lap. If you'd like to accept it, then simply read on and follow the steps outlined in this book. The decision is yours to make. Flip the page and open a new chapter in your life—The chapter on Senior Living Investing.

PART 1

WHAT YOU NEED TO KNOW ABOUT SENIOR LIVING

Chapter 1

What is Senior Living?

People who have never been exposed to Western culture often find themselves confused at the prospect of "Senior Living." Even within Western culture, there are varied opinions regarding the ethical aspects of moving elderly individuals into facilities where they are isolated from other members of their families and only receive periodic visits. However, this perception could not be more incorrect.

When one takes the time to research and truly understand the nuances of Senior Living, the benefits of seniors living together as a group tends to come to light quickly. Rather than being a method of diverting the responsibility of caring for the elderly, Senior Living homes give our loved ones an environment where they can receive the around-the-clock attention and care they need in comfortable "home-like" surroundings.

Senior Living is a term often used to describe housing and care options for older adults. These housing options may range from independent living communities, which provide a social and active lifestyle for older adults who don't need much assistance, to residential assisted living (RAL) facilities, which offer more support and care for seniors who need help with daily tasks like dressing, bathing, and medication management. Other types of Senior Living options may include skilled nursing facilities for seniors who require round-the-clock medical care and memory care units for those with Alzheimer's disease or other forms

of Dementia.

Senior Living also encompasses the services and amenities provided within these housing options, such as meal preparation, transportation, housekeeping, and social and recreational activities to promote the physical, emotional, and mental well-being of older adults.

1

That said, there are two major reasons Senior Living homes provide better lives for the elderly than they would otherwise receive at home:

- First, you must consider the medical aspect of their care. For aging individuals, having well-equipped living quarters and medical personnel is a necessity. It is nearly impossible for a typical family to be adequately equipped and able to deal with long-term senior healthcare issues. Senior Living homes, on the other hand, afford the aging population a chance to live out the remainder of their lives with other, similarly aged members of their community and in spaces where their medical and personal care needs are met.

- Secondly, it is essential to consider the aging individual's state of mind. Being in a senior care facility often allows them a more emotionally pleasant experience than they would experience staying with a family member. After all, it's easy to feel negative emotions like guilt and regret when you actively see the strain your presence is placing on a loved one. In Senior Living homes, however, the residents understand that the staff *wants* to be there taking care of them. This allows for a more pleasant living situation than the alternative.

Why Do People Need Senior Housing?

There are many reasons why one may consider looking into Senior Living options for themselves or a loved one:

- **Safety:** Senior Living communities are designed with safety in mind and often have features such as emergency call systems, grab bars in bathrooms, and non-slip flooring to prevent falls and other accidents.

- **Assistance with daily tasks:** Senior Living communities offer varying levels of assistance with daily tasks, from housekeeping and meal preparation to assistance with bathing and dressing. This can help seniors maintain their independence and quality of life.

- **Socialization:** Isolation and loneliness can be significant issues for older adults, especially those who live alone. Senior Living communities provide opportunities for socialization and companionship, with activities and events designed to encourage social interaction and community engagement.

- **Access to healthcare:** Many Senior Living communities offer on-site healthcare services, such as nursing care, medication management, and rehabilitation services. This can be especially beneficial for seniors with chronic health conditions.

- **Peace of mind for loved ones:** When an older adult moves into a Senior Living community, their loved ones can have peace of mind knowing that they are receiving the care and support they need. This can help to alleviate stress and worry for family members and caregivers.

Overall, Senior Living can provide a safe, supportive, and engaging environment for older adults, with a range of services and amenities designed to enhance their quality of life.

Senior Living Categories

Now that you have a good understanding of the numbers, it's time to investigate what Senior Living is all about.

That said, most retirement homes fall into four categories:

Independent Living

Independent living is common for active seniors who are still able-bodied but would prefer to live in a community with others. In homes like these, the Senior Living facility looks and functions like an apartment complex (with some additions, of course). It's also common for staff members to have only basic medical training.

With homes such as these, you can expect to see "apartments" connected by interior hallways that are equipped with various railings and mobility aids. It's also common for these complexes to have easy-to-use laundry facilities and common rooms where residents can mingle. There may even be an optional communal cafeteria for those who do not wish to cook their own food, although the units will typically have kitchens.

Assisted Living

Assisted living is more like what one typically thinks of as a retirement home for seniors with medical conditions or physical ailments that require regular medical attention. In this type of home, the living quarters may still resemble apartments, but they will also be much more catered to ease of use for both staff and residents. For example, most beds will have detachable railings, and toilets with handrails, etc.

Additionally, the staff in these homes will have been specially trained to deal with common senior ailments such as Alzheimer's or Dementia and are much closer to nursing staff than regular apartment staff.

These homes will also have stricter rules than the independent living facilities to maintain the well-being of their residents. For example, some units may not come with dangerous items like stoves. Some rooms may even have cameras installed in them to monitor the resident. However, this usually only happens at the family's request or if the staff considers it necessary.

Skilled Nursing Home

Skilled nursing homes are what most people think of when they hear the term "senior housing." In these homes, seniors with severe health conditions or who need 24-hour supervision may reside and live comfortably.

These homes contain 24/7 qualified medical practitioners looking after the health and well-being of the residents. Skilled nursing homes also cater to people who are not necessarily elderly but require constant medical attention to help cure, curb, or recover from an injury or major surgery.

In these types of homes, however, the resident may have less freedom than independent and assisted living and may not be allowed to perform certain tasks. Everything in skilled nursing homes is dedicated to maintaining resident safety, so they tend to be more restrictive than other alternatives.

Memory Care

Memory care facilities provide much of the same care that RAL facilities do. The primary difference between them is that memory care facilities provide extra support for those with memory-related issues such as Dementia, Alzheimer's, or general cognitive decline.

Some of the additional provisions include things like increased caregiver presences, wearable tracking devices, controlled building access, door alarms, etc. All of these things are specially designed with resident safety in mind.

Hospice/Palliative Care

This is another type of senior care that is rarely mentioned in discussions about Senior Living because it usually takes place in non-senior-specific facilities or at the senior's home:

When a senior reaches what medical professionals expect to be the end of his/her life, they are placed in hospice or palliative care. This service is also sometimes provided to terminally ill people who might not be a senior.

Hospice usually takes place in the individual's home, where they can be in the presence of their loved ones. Sometimes, however, assisted living facilities provide hospice care on-site to support the individuals under their care.

Home-hospice nursing assistance is typically only provided if the home is a satisfactory place for the individual to spend their final days. Hospice usually includes a variety of services to ensure the individual is comfortable, such as social, spiritual, and physical support as needed.

Palliative care is mostly the same as hospice but does have some key differences. Where hospice is restricted to end-of-life situations, palliative care can begin from the point of diagnosis or once treatment starts. In other words, palliative care is carried out at the same time as treatment, while hospice begins only once treatment has stopped and it is clear the individual likely won't survive the illness.

Key Takeaways

Now that you know the types of Senior Living facilities, let's explore why they make a good investment.

Chapter 2

The "Why" of Senior Living Investing

Why Invest In Senior Living?

If you're anything like us, you want to gather all the information you can before deciding to invest in Senior Living. But you don't just want someone to **tell** you; instead, you want real, measurable figures you can use to compare this sector with others.

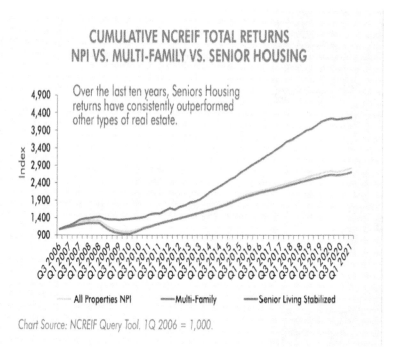

CUMULATIVE NCREIF TOTAL RETURNS
NPI VS. MULTI-FAMILY VS. SENIOR HOUSING

Over the last ten years, Seniors Housing returns have consistently outperformed other types of real estate.

All Properties NPI · Multi-Family · Senior Living Stabilized

Chart Source: NCREIF Query Tool. 1Q 2006 = 1,000.

According to the NCREIF Query Tool, the returns from Senior Living investments have been greater than that of multi-family and the rest of the commercial real estate market (represented by All Properties NPI).

Over the last decade, both of the latter real estate sectors have performed as expected: aside from a significant dip during the 2008 housing crisis, there has been a steady increase in total returns across the board. For multi-family properties, the average ROI is 6.10%; for the general commercial real estate market, this number sits at 6.09%.

As you can see in the chart, however, Senior Living real estate has far outpaced all other real estate sectors in the industry. Not only did it do much better at withstanding the 2008 housing market crash, but it also recovered more quickly from the COVID-19 pandemic and grew at a much greater rate over the course of ten years. Currently, the average ROI on Senior Living real estate sits at 10.52%.

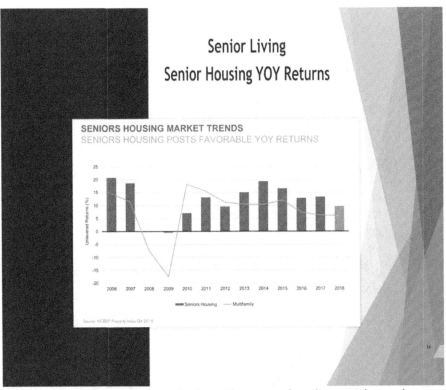

Of course, we understand that those unfamiliar with real estate investment might not consider those numbers to be all-that-groundbreaking. However, when looking at real estate returns, it's important to apply industry statistics to potential investment scenarios for the best understanding of what you stand to gain as an investor in a particular asset class.

www.VinneyChopra.com/FreeBenefits

Investing in Senior Living can be a wise financial decision for several reasons:

- **Growing demand**: The senior population is growing rapidly, and this trend is expected to continue for the foreseeable future. As more Baby Boomers reach retirement age, the demand for Senior Living options is expected to increase.
- **Recession-resistant**: Senior Living is a recession-resistant industry, as the need for care services does not decrease during economic downturns. In fact, the demand for Senior Living options may increase during times of economic uncertainty as families may seek out affordable, safe, and supportive options for their loved ones.
- **Stable income streams**: Senior Living investments can provide steady income streams for investors, as many Senior Living communities operate on a lease model. This means that investors can receive consistent rental income from their properties.
- **Potential for capital appreciation**: The value of Senior Living properties may appreciate over time, especially if they are in desirable areas with high demand for Senior Living options.
- **Social impact**: This is the HUGE ELEMENT in my thinking and what got me excited and motivated to invest in Senior Living as my way of "paying it forward." Investing in Senior Living can have a positive social impact by supporting the care and well-being of older adults. This can be a rewarding way to invest capital while making a positive difference in the lives of others.

Overall, investing in Senior Living can be a smart financial decision for those looking for stable income streams, the potential for capital appreciation, and a socially impactful investment opportunity.

Senior Housing Is Easily Overlooked By Investors

The Senior Living market is often overlooked by investors, despite all the data that points to the enormous opportunities, primarily because many investors don't understand it. Investments in this sector are more profitable than putting money into college housing or all-age multi-family properties.

Why? Modern medicine has increased the life expectancy of elderly citizens, meaning residents will live in these homes longer than they used to, paying more rent and providing more profit to investors, with many living in the same place until they no longer can. Conversely, the student housing market is fixed, and its residents are more transient, flowing in and out of temporary living environments each year. In contrast, multi-family residents in all-age properties often move within just a few years.

We Cannot Overlook the Shortage of Senior Housing

Senior housing demand is here to stay due to unprecedented growth in demographics.

Here is a detailed explanation of how the changing demographics and demand are contributing to a shortage of senior housing in the USA for many years to come:

Demographic changes, including the aging of the Baby Boomer generation, have led to an increased demand for senior housing in the United States. According to a report by the National Investment Center for Seniors Housing & Care, the number of Americans aged 80 and over is expected to increase from 12 million in 2020 to nearly 19 million by 2030, a 58% increase. As a result, the demand for senior housing options is greater than ever before.

www.VinneyChopra.com/FreeBenefits

However, the supply of Senior Living options is struggling to keep up with the demand. This is due to a combination of factors:

- First, the Baby Boomer generation, born between 1946 and 1964, representing the second largest generation in U.S. history (after Millennials), is now reaching retirement age.
- Second, advances in medical technology and healthcare have extended the average lifespan, leading to an increase in the vast number of seniors who require specialized care.
- Third, there is a growing trend among seniors to downsize their homes and move into smaller, more manageable living arrangements; this means that seniors are increasingly seeking out Senior Living communities, assisted living facilities, and other types of specialized housing designed to meet their unique and changing needs.
- Fourth, developers have been slow to build new senior housing communities due to costly land acquisition and construction, permitting challenges, and other barriers to entry.
- Fifth, there is a shortage of skilled workers to care for seniors.

The result is a shortage of senior housing across the country. In some states, such as Florida, the demand for senior housing is so high that occupancy rates have reached nearly 98%.

The shortage is compounded by a lack of affordable options. Senior housing can be expensive, and Medicare does not typically cover the cost of assisted living or memory care. Many seniors are living in inadequate or unsafe housing simply because they cannot afford to move into a Senior Living community.

The shortage of affordable senior housing is expected to persist for many years to come. The National Investment Center for Seniors Housing & Care predicts that senior housing supply will fall short of demand by approximately 320,000 units in 2025 and by as much as 2.5 million units by 2040. This will continue to put pressure on seniors and their families to find safe, affordable housing options as they age. As demand continues to grow and supply struggles to keep up, seniors may find themselves facing long waitlists for housing or may be forced to pay exorbitant prices for the care they need.

Policymakers and industry leaders must work together to address this issue and ensure that seniors have access to the affordable housing and care they need to live healthy, fulfilling lives in their golden years.

As previously discussed, as of 2023, the United States is undergoing an unprecedented demographic shift, with the population of older adults rapidly increasing. In fact, by 2030, there will be an estimated 78 million Americans over the age of 65, representing nearly 20% of the total population. This demographic shift, often referred to as the **"Silver Tsunami,"** is already having a profound impact on the senior housing market in the United States, with demand for senior housing far outpacing available supply.

Many older adults are looking for housing options that allow them to "age in place," meaning they can live independently for as long as possible. However, these options are often limited, particularly in urban areas where housing costs are high, and space is at a premium. Additionally, there is a shortage of skilled nursing facilities and other forms of assisted living, which are often necessary for older adults who require higher levels of care.

The shortage of senior housing is not only problematic for older adults and their families but also for the economy. Without adequate housing options, older adults may be reluctant to downsize or move to a more suitable living situation, leading to a decline in home sales and a stagnation of the real estate market.

Additionally, if more and more older adults require specialized care that can only be accessed through off-site medical facilities, there will be a growing burden on the overall healthcare system, with an increased demand for medical professionals and resources.

One potential solution to this problem is to increase the supply of senior housing that includes differing levels of medical care. This could reduce the burden on the general healthcare system for medical conditions related to seniors who inconsistently administer their own medication or for minor conditions that can be handled by in-house or visiting professionals.

Incentives to increase the senior housing supply can be accomplished through a variety of means, such as incentivizing developers to build more Senior Living communities, offering tax breaks or subsidies to providers of senior care, and improving access to financing and capital for senior housing providers.

Projected Increases In The Number Of Seniors

By 2035, the United States is projected to have more seniors than young people. The members of this massive groundswell have been labeled the "silver tsunami."

This is not an unexpected event, however. This significant increase in the senior population is due to the generation known as Baby Boomers reaching their senior years during a period that is currently being referred to as the "Baby Bust," where millennials have fewer and fewer children each year. Because of this, there is a quickly increasing gap in the number of seniors versus the number of young adults.

By 2050, countries across the world will see an escalating rise in their senior populations, which will lead to changes and challenges that cut across all sectors of the economy, including real estate and investing practices. Viewed in this light, affordable, comfortable senior housing units are not a luxury but rather a standardized requirement for an aging population's quality of life.

With the anticipated expanding demand for Senior Living housing, supply will have to catch up. Today, we can see Senior Living communities popping up all over the country. Even cultures that encourage their seniors to live at home are building separate living accommodations to ensure their elderly loved ones have a top-tier quality of life. Senior Living residences must stand out – The elderly living environments of today far exceed the quality of those of the past. Seniors want convenience, unrivaled care, attention, amenities, comfort, aesthetics, and more.

In a recent interview with CityAge.com, architect Daniel Libeskind said,

"My idea is not to treat the elderly as if they are old. Treat them as if they are young. Give them an environment that is uplifting. Create social spaces and atriums ... Create something that says, 'This is an environment that is positive.'

Projected Increases In Care Requirements

Recent studies in the United States predict that cases of Alzheimer's will increase by 2050 in accordance with the number of seniors. And because of the increased number of elders per family, many families will likely struggle with the financial and emotional burden that comes with their care.

Additionally, while proper nutrition and exercise might create circumstances in which the elderly can more adequately care for themselves for longer, it will not reverse the flow of time. Aging is inevitable, and Senior Living housing is the first step to a better quality of life, both for seniors and their family members.

Demand Is Driven By A Convergence Of Factors

The numbers are staggering. The Baby Boomer generation is well on its way to retirement — if they're not there already — and the market will soon be saturated with people who have outpaced the number of residences available.

With investments, there's never a single factor that causes the demand for a particular sector to explode. Senior Living real estate is no exception to this rule, and Baby Boomers alone aren't enough to have caused the massive increase in demand for Senior Living facilities. So then, what other factors are playing into this unprecedented spike in demand?

Perhaps the second largest contributor to our current situation, aside from the Baby Boomers, is the growing expectation of longevity in the elderly. At the turn of the century, the United Nations proclaimed that "longevity is the greatest social transformation of this era," and they were right. Not only are there more and more seniors in need of housing, but the length of time that housing is occupied by a particular resident is continually climbing.

According to renowned biologist Tom Kirkwood, "If death is a finish line, that line has continually moved farther and farther away over the past century." In the mid-nineteenth century, better public health measures, including clean drinking water, improved sanitation, and the widespread use of vaccines, led to an increase in overall life expectancy.

According to Statista.com, the average life expectancy in 1950 (a mere 70 years ago) was 67. Today, that number has risen to 78 years, and the trend shows no sign of abating.

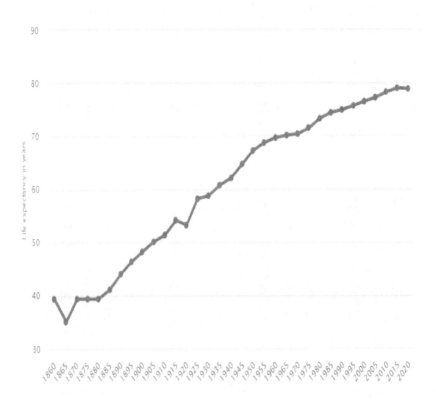

(From Statista.com)

Now, we are in an aging crisis, with more seniors than facilities to accommodate them and longer life spans than ever before in history., Yet, despite the increased demand, or perhaps because of it, nearly 3 million low-income seniors cannot find affordable housing.

Benefits of Senior Living Investing

The Senior Living investing space has become a booming market. It is a captive market with potential buyers and occupants, regardless of the type of Senior Living facility you invest in.

Previously, the United States Department of Housing and Urban Development (HUD) and certain jurisdictions (such as California) have passed regulations making it easier for homeowners to build smaller, secondary housing units on their property as one means of addressing the senior housing crisis, but this is a band-aid solution to a hemorrhaging market. Previous efforts haven't made a dent in addressing the growing number of elderly residents without a safe, appropriate, and affordable place to live.

Because of this, there is arguably no better investment (real estate or otherwise) than Senior Living homes.

Benefits For Seniors

Are affordable, high-quality residences for seniors even possible? You, as an investor, may be asking yourself this exact question. In short, the answer is a resounding "Yes!"

The demand for Senior Living homes has created a unique situation where any price set at or below the market average will always result in full or almost-full housing. Because of the demand, a return on investment in Senior Living properties is nearly guaranteed. Another consideration is that many of the amenity costs a Senior Living facility incurs will be one-time expenses, yet the investment will continue to generate income over the lifespan of the project.

As a result, investing in Senior Living homes is generally both financially sound and morally gratifying.

Tax Benefits For Investors

Yes, there are tax benefits associated with investing in Senior Living. However, the tax benefits you or your investing partners may realize will depend on the specific investment structure and each investor's tax situation. Here are a few examples of potential tax benefits:

- Depreciation: Investors may be able to take advantage of depreciation deductions on a Senior Living property, which can help reduce their taxable income.

- **Capital gains tax**: If an investor holds their Senior Living investment for more than a year (most are multi-year investments), they may qualify for long-term capital gains tax rates, which are generally lower than short-term rates.
- **Opportunity zones**: Some Senior Living projects may be in Opportunity Zones, designated geographic areas that offer tax incentives for investors who invest in those areas. If an investor reinvests its capital gains from any source (it doesn't have to be real estate) in a Senior Living property located in an Opportunity Zone, they may be able to defer paying capital gains tax on the sale, and they may additionally be entitled to certain increases in their cost basis (a "step-up") based on the value of their Opportunity Zone investment at the end of a specified holding period.
- **1031 exchanges**: A 1031 exchange is a tax-deferred exchange of one investment property for another. If an investor sells other real estate and purchases a Senior Living property within a specified timeframe, they may be able to defer paying capital gains tax on the sale under the United States Internal Revenue Service's 1031 Exchange rules.

It's important to note that tax laws and regulations are subject to change, and investors should consult with a tax professional to fully understand the potential tax benefits and implications of investing in Senior Living.

Is It Easy To Invest In Senior Living?

Investing in Senior Living can be complex, but it can be made easier with sufficient knowledge and resources. Here are some factors to consider when investing in Senior Living:

www.VinneyChopra.com/FreeBenefits

- **Access to information:** Before investing, it's important to conduct thorough research to understand the market and the specific Senior Living project. Investors should look for information on the demographics of the area, the demand for Senior Living, the quality of the property, and the reputation of the developer or operator.

- **Define your investment goals:** Determine what you hope to achieve through your investment in Senior Living. Are you looking for steady cash flow, long-term appreciation, or a combination of both?

- **Understanding the investment structure:** There are various investment structures available for investing in Senior Living. Each structure has its own advantages and disadvantages, and investors should understand the structure they are investing in to make informed decisions. Options include:
  - Direct ownership and operation,
  - Passively investing in a Senior Living Syndicate formed to develop or acquire a specific project,
  - Passively investing in a Senior Living Fund formed to develop and/or acquire multiple Senior Living properties, and
  - Joint ventures with operators and/or other investors where everyone is actively involved in generating their own profits.

- **Working with experienced partners:** Investing in Senior Living can be complex, so it's important to work with experienced partners such as developers, operators, and investment managers who have a proven track record in the industry.

- **Evaluate potential investments:** Once you have identified potential Senior Living investment opportunities, evaluate them thoroughly. Look for information on the quality of the property, the reputation of the developer or operator, and the financials of the specific investment.

- **Managing risks:** As with any investment, there are risks associated with investing in Senior Living, including regulatory and legal risks, operational risks, and market risks. Investors should carefully evaluate these risks and work with their active partners or rely on their experienced management team to develop strategies to manage them and to keep them informed of their progress.

- **Consult with a financial advisor and/or tax professional**: Before making any investment, it's important to consult with a financial advisor and/or tax professional to ensure that the investment aligns with your overall financial plan and to understand the potential tax implications of the investment.

Overall, investing in Senior Living can be a rewarding opportunity for investors who are willing to do their due diligence and work with experienced developers and operators; or those willing to learn the Senior Living business and actively own and operate Senior Living facilities themselves.

While it requires doing your own research as to whether investing in Senior Living is a good fit for you, with the right resources and support, you can navigate the complexities of the Senior Living market and make informed investment decisions.

The Time Is Now

With all these elements in place, the time to get in on the ground floor, ahead of other investors, is now. The annualized ROI for passive investors in senior housing has steadily held at 13% yearly, which is staggering for most markets. You can maintain that advantage with this massive — and passive — earning potential.

The question remains: Where should you invest in Senior Living? The short answer is that it depends on several factors. In the following section, we will show you a feasibility study and financial breakdown. We'll also look at what things buyers and investors look at before investing in Senior Living projects.

Chapter 3

Senior Living Business Models

Primary Types of Senior Living Housing

According to existing research, nearly 90 percent of seniors aged 65+ prefer to "age in place." Aging in place is a concept that describes when a senior ages while staying in the same location (whether at home or in a facility) for the remainder of their life. At the same time, research also dictates that nearly 70% of the population will require long-term senior care at some point in their later lives.

Regardless of preference, though, those who must live in senior housing (whether by their choice or not) agree on one general fact: they'd like the place to feel like home.

Consider your own preferences for when you travel. Perhaps you like to stay in boho-chic Airbnbs that feel like a home away from home. Or maybe you like upscale hotels with rooftop dining and a 24-hour pool. Then again, perhaps you prefer to vacation in a vehicle you can take with you, like an RV or a boat.

It's important to realize that these preferences don't go away just because we age and aren't able to express them as clearly (or choose them for ourselves). Because of these differences in preference, there are a variety of business models that have been created to cater to the different "types" of seniors seeking long-term care.

Let's explore the types of housing facilities currently available to seniors:

Continuous Care (Age In Place) Retirement Community (CCRC)

A continuous care retirement community (CCRC) is a type of independent living facility dedicated to providing a place for seniors to age without ever forcing them to relocate to better suit their needs. In other words, the facility delegates its resources so that it can properly handle seniors at all stages of life, resulting in a type of facility that can take care of seniors throughout the entire aging process.

This sounds confusing, so let's break it down:

With CCRCs, a certain percentage of resident rooms are reserved for higher levels of care. Approximately 60% are reserved for seniors who can still function relatively independently. The other 40% is split between assisted living services (about 25%) and those needing memory care or hospice services (about 15%).

By using this business model, residents can move up in the levels of care as they need it. This type of age-in-place model is popular in today's Senior Living marketplace because it caters to most senior preferences. Because of this, the model helps increase resident retention compared to other models.

According to a recent report from investment firm CBRE, the model not only definitely works but also helps maintain a degree of resident regularity. The report effectively demonstrates how, even in situations where other segments of Senior Living have experienced economy-related dips in residency, CCRCs maintained their typical, *static* 91% average occupancy rate.

Furthermore, CCRCs are not intended for seniors to enter the system at the later stages of life (such as when they already need assisted care). The intention is to enter the system early while they can still live independently and remain there for the rest of their lives.

In this model, there may be a sizable entrance fee (usually between $200,000 to $700,000) to ensure the resident is committed to remaining there and aging through the system. The fee may be held by the facility and returned at the end of the senior's life to the next of kin. The amount returned can be anywhere from 0% to 90%, depending on how long the resident remained at the facility, among other contractual stipulations. Then, while living at the facility, there is also a monthly fee based on how much care the senior needs, ranging from $3,000 to $8,000/month. The monthly fee also depends on the geographic area the facility is in and competing Senior Living facilities.

Independent, Assisted, And Memory Care Facilities (IL/AL/MC)

IL/AL/MC facilities are developed to mimic the look and feel of a hotel while providing plenty of space to house multiple residents. These facilities may have anywhere between 50 and 300 rooms spread across multiple floors.

Each room is built to mimic a mini-suite and usually ranges between 300 and 600 square feet in size. The space typically includes a bed, private bathroom, and kitchenette (in certain rooms). These facilities also may have long hallways with movement-assist bars to help residents get around, as well as elevators and a cafeteria.

The biggest difference between these types of facilities and CCRC is that these do not charge hefty up-front fees for admission. Instead, they have one-time "new resident move-in fees," much like the deposit you would pay if you were renting an apartment or home. These fees are usually between $1,000 and $2,500, depending on the level of care the senior needs and the level of comfort the facility provides. Once that is paid, the facility will charge a monthly fee, like rent, between $3,000 and $15,000.

As you've likely already gathered, the level of care a senior needs heavily influences how much their stay will cost. Usually, the levels of care are separated into three unique tiers—where each new tier of care results in a higher pricing structure.

Furthermore, IL/AL/MC facilities are also designed to be able to accommodate the continuous care structure we mentioned before. Many of them are also equipped with upscale amenities like community rooms, indoor movie theaters, on-site libraries, large dining rooms, hair and nail salons, etc. Most will also provide excursions (for a fee) and a shuttle to local grocery stores, etc.

These facilities are ideal for the senior who is still primarily independent and would like to secure all their housing needs ahead of time and have the option to receive additional care later down the line without being forced to transfer facilities.

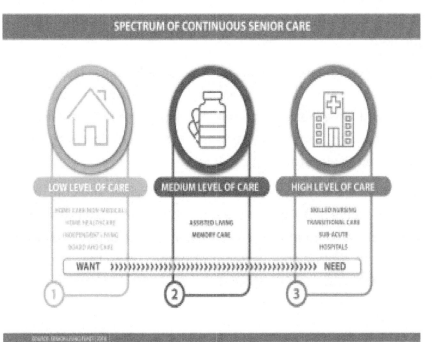

Residential Assisted Living Facilities (RAL)

This is the type of care facility you'll hear about the most in this book. A small, upscale, private-pay environment, this type of Senior Living home is quickly becoming one of the most preferred options for elderly individuals needing around-the-clock care. Usually, this is done in single-family-style homes in residential neighborhoods or in a group of residential-style homes specifically built to look like a residential community.

This type of care facility gives the residents a feeling of being at home while ensuring they have access to the care they need. Most often, the home will look just like a normal house with small modifications made to support the elderly individuals living there. The home will have anywhere from 8-16 private bedrooms (many with their own private bathrooms) and will have several members of staff that cycle throughout the day.

This home environment is great because it provides a better-than-average caregiver-to-resident ratio for the best care experience. Typically, you'll see these types of facilities have a five-to-one caregiver-to-resident ratio. This means there are plenty of staff members to help with cleaning, cooking, medication management, bathing, toileting, and other personal needs. Many of them also provide rooms or nearby houses where families can visit their loved ones in peace.

Cluster Home Senior Care Facilities (CHSC)

A new favorite among investors is the cluster home senior care facility model. This model is praised for its economic scalability as it creates a new way to build multiple senior residential centers in a single development project or locale.

With a cluster home design, multiple senior care facilities are built to share a plot of land and are usually centered around shared outdoor amenities. Some of the most common amenities for CHSC homes are ponds, walking trails, on-site beauty salons, outdoor sitting areas, gorgeous landscaping, etc.

Utilizing this type of facility layout provides residents with unique activity opportunities. Rather than having to partner with other sources for outdoor senior activities, an onsite staff member is able to plan, control, and execute them. This generally opens seniors up to new activities like bird watching, swimming, walking, gardening, etc.

This type of facility also majorly benefits investors. By building a Senior Living facility in home clusters, you can create economic efficiencies that other Senior Living types can't match.

Furthermore, some of these cluster developments have taken to combining independent living, assisted living, and memory care facilities on the same site but in different buildings to provide different levels of care more effectively than other models.

An example of a complete CHSC facility would be a cluster of buildings that include around fifteen independent living townhomes, four 12-bedroom assisted living homes, two 10-bedroom memory care homes, additional cottages for family visits, a beauty salon, a central dining hall, and a "main facility" where activities can be held, among other things.

Shared Common Space Independent Living

Another common preference for seniors is a configuration of townhomes, apartments, cottages, or villas where fully independent individuals can live together in a one-fee living arrangement. With this arrangement, everyone has their own private bedroom (with some having a private bath), and common areas are shared.

This type of facility has proven to have strong cash flow because only minimal staff is required, and the primary capital investment is the amount needed to build and equip the facility.

Affordability and Payment

If there's one obvious thing about senior care, it can be *expensive*. When a senior reaches the point that 24/7 care is required, the family can often no longer provide the necessary level of care. The family (and the senior) must choose between private home health care or a shared living facility.

Let's look at how each of these breaks down in terms of cost:

- **Private Home Healthcare.** For most home healthcare agencies, the average hourly rate for a skilled caregiver is $25 to $28. And since this person is needed every day for an average of 8 hours a day, we multiply this amount by approximately 30 days per month ($25 x 8 hours a day x 30 days a month). Doing the math, the family would spend about $6,000 per month on in-home care this way. Alternatively, they could hire a full-time live-in caregiver for around $200 a day, which also comes to $6,000 a month. No matter how you view it, at-home senior care is expensive.

- **Shared Living Facility.** This is where Senior Living comes in. Oftentimes, it's cheaper than in-home care—and much less stressful than having a stranger in your house. However, this doesn't mean it's cheap. One of the most prominent issues the Senior Living industry faces is the issue of affordability. That's why each of the above housing models has both private pay and public assisted housing varieties. Private pay will be naturally more expensive but of higher quality, while public assistance will be more affordable but is often less maintained with fewer amenities.

As an operator/investor, part of your job is to find a happy medium that will best serve your community and allow you to create and provide (or invest in) your preferred Senior Living model.

PART 2

HOW TO BE AN ACTIVE INVESTOR

Chapter 4

Actively Investing in Senior Living

Whether you are considering Senior Living as an active or passive investment, reading all of the information in this book will help you become a better-informed investor.

To maximize the profit potential of any new investment opportunity, you want to dive in only after you are well-informed. Additionally, should other potential investors consider pledging funds to your cause, you want to be able to answer their questions and establish that you know what you're doing. Reading this book in full before you start will help you be able to do that.

Even if you want to be a passive investor, don't skip ahead, as you should understand what an active investor you might invest with should be doing to effectively acquire, create, and manage a Senior Living investment. This way, you'll be able to ask sufficient questions and stay informed about operational challenges and successes your investment property generates.

Now, on the topic of being well-educated, let's start from the beginning:

What Is Active Investment?

For new investors, there will likely be some confusion around this concept. After all, investing is investing, right?

Well, not exactly.

As with anything, investing is a topic with many subcategories and various ways you can invest in any one thing. Active investing and passive investing are merely two of those options.

The best way to explain how active and passive investing are different is to look at an example:

33

Let's say that you want to invest in a hardware store. You know a lot about the topic, and there aren't many hardware stores in your area. It looks like an excellent prospect.

Now, however, you must decide how you are going to go about investing in that hardware store. Are you going to seek financial backers, rent a building, purchase inventory, and run the business yourself? Or will you merely provide funding to an already existing or soon-to-exist hardware store operator in exchange for being a shareholder in the company?

The first option is an example of active investing. It's hands-on and puts most of the power and decisions regarding that business directly in your hands. The second option is passive investing, which we'll discuss later.

Active investors are those who prefer to buy an existing Senior Living establishment or develop a new one from the ground up. If you are an active investor, acquiring and overseeing operations at your project may consume as much time as a full-time job as you actively manage the various aspects of one or more Senior Living homes.

The active investor is characterized by their hands-on approach to all business-related activities. This means being on-site during the week, creating standard operating procedures, and making day-to-day decisions as your Senior Living business's president or Chief Executive Officer.

In simplified form, you can think of it like this: active investors operate in a capacity like the president or manager of a business, whereas passive investors operate in a more shareholder-like capacity.

In the following parts of this book, we'll cover the duties and due diligence required of each type of investor. We will also explore how precisely you can get started in Senior Living investment, depending on which type of investor you wish to be.

Regardless of whether you have already made up your mind, we highly recommend reading both the Active and Passive Investor portions of this book to gain a breadth of knowledge on the subject and be better able to make an informed decision about which investing type and which Senior Living category is the best fit for you. For active investors, reading the passive section will help you determine your investors' motivation (or lack of motivation) to invest with you.

Some of you may wish to skip one or the other section. Although you may miss out on valuable information, doing so will ultimately not affect your ability to use the information to begin your investment journey.

Hands-On or Hands-Off?

As the business owner, you oversee high-level business operations, although you might hire an operator or manager to be responsible for the day-to-day operations. While you should always know what goes on in your business, you should ideally spend most of your time working *on* your business rather than *in* it, but how involved you are will depend entirely on your capacity and desire.

Running A Hands-Off Elder Care Home

If you've decided to remain hands-off in the day-to-day operations of your business, you will need to ensure that:

- You've accurately delegated roles and hired the right people, including caregivers, managerial staff, and a maintenance crew.
- Don't hover. Spend less time in the facility and more time making your business better. Let your manager be your eyes and ears.
- Train your staff properly. This includes encouraging training sessions and offering opportunities for ongoing education in their related field.

Doing these things can be especially difficult for new business owners as you want to ensure your facility is up to par. However, you hire an experienced manager for a reason, and you should practice stepping back and allowing them to manage.

That said, we aren't saying you should be completely hands-off. There is always the possibility that, no matter how upstanding your manager or member of your staff may seem, they aren't adhering to necessary operating procedures. This could be intentional or unintentional, but it's vital that you try to ensure this isn't a recurrent issue to avoid potential lawsuits or even criminal charges.

To prevent this, we recommend doing surprise inspections every so often to ensure things are going according to plan. You may even consider sending someone undercover to get information your staff wouldn't normally reveal.

Running A Hands-On Elder Care Home

As you may have guessed, with a hands-on approach, you will be present at your facility much more often. You may take on the role of a general manager in addition to being the veritable CEO.

Your daily tasks may include things like:

- Meeting with managers to discuss expectations.
- Looking over accounting reports to determine the best financial course for your facility.
- Interviewing and hiring new managers for your facility.
- Handling important complaints from residents.
- Managing staff schedules.
- Monitoring resident care.
- Heading care management meetings.
- Identifying training needs and updating standard operating procedures (SOPs).
- Overseeing advertisement and marketing of the facility.

- Reviewing and correcting problematic policies.
- Reporting to regulators and ensuring adherence to regulations.
- Auditing care plans and medication records.
- Reviewing staff performance.

The Most Important Aspect of Active Investment

As you may have guessed, active investment is much more complicated than passively investing in a Senior Living project. It requires more knowledge in the area, more time, and self-funding. In exchange, however, you can often gain a greater return on your investment than you would if you had to share profits with investors.

However, the most critical aspect of active investment is having a solid investor base or enough money to fund a desired project on your own.

With passive investment, you can invest as much money as you wish. You may get a return on that money, or you may not, but you aren't responsible if the business fails, and you don't have to devote the time needed to be an owner/operator of your Senior Living business.

As an active investor, you will often own all or part of the company you are investing in, but you will always be in control and responsible for business operations. You will be the 100% owner of the company if you only invest your own money. If you include other investors, you may sell ownership interests in your company to them, or you may simply offer them a share of the cash flow and/or profits as a fixed return. Your investors could be active in the business with you, or they could be passive investors.

By building up a solid passive investor base that trusts in your expertise and can provide you with funds when you need them, you can vastly decrease your odds of failure; and you will retain control of the company as you operate it on your investors' behalf.

As an active investor, you could operate the business, own the real estate, or do both.

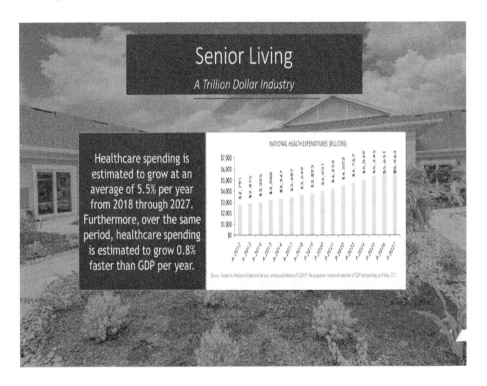

Generating an ROI is Key to Attracting Investors

A return on investment (ROI) measures how much profit is made from an investment compared to how much cash is invested. If you plan to bring in passive investors to fund your Senior Living business, your investors will expect you to generate profit that you can share with them. You must ensure your Senior Living home is operating at a profit so that you can pay periodic distributions from cash flow and eventual resale to investors, and you must also generate sufficient profit to pay yourself and your other active partners.

www.VinneyChopra.com/FreeBenefits

Balancing Affordability With Investor Returns

Assuming you are choosing to Senior Living investment out of equal parts opportunity and a desire to help people, you'll need to keep it affordable to the local population.

So, with that in mind, how do you increase your revenue without directly increasing the price and pricing yourself out of the market so that occupancy dips?

The answer is simple: increase your resident volume. This can be achieved by adding beds to an existing facility and ensuring that your monthly rates are commensurate with what local residents can afford to pay as they transition from living in their own homes to your Senior Living facility.

In the first quarter of 2021 (because of the Covid pandemic), senior housing occupancy reached a record low of 78.8 percent. This was down 1.8 percentage points from the previous quarter and *8.7 percentage points from only a year earlier.* (<u>National Investment Center for Seniors Housing and Care, 2022</u>)

Let's break down what a dip like that means for you in terms of profit:

Let's say that you have ten individual living quarters in your Senior Living facility. Let's also say that you charge an affordable price, around $2200 per month (well below the national average).

80% occupancy would mean that you consistently have eight rooms filled out of those 10, leaving two empty each month. At $2200 per month per resident, having two empty living quarters would cost you *$4,400 per month.*

That's almost $53,000 annually. In the residential assisted living space, $53,000 can make a massive difference in whether you have profits to share with investors.

To maximize your resident occupancy rates, you should always ensure that your Senior Living homes are:

- Situated in a community where the residents are accessible to family members;
- There should be access to public transportation; and
- The property should be accessible to the greater social environment, including activities, events, grocery stores, places of worship, restaurants, salons, etc.

Accessibility will make your Senior Living homes more attractive and increase the occupancy rate, directly impacting cash flow and your ability to attract investors.

Ultimately, you want to charge what the market will bear for your services and living accommodations, regardless of how many seniors occupy it. But if you're priced out of the market, your rooms — and the pockets of your investors (which could mean yours) — may remain empty.

This is where you're marketing and knowledge of the audience comes into play. If your Senior Living property offers amenities, comfort and places the dignity of potential residents above all, you'll appeal to a wider audience. The seniors in your area might be reluctant to leave their homes and give up the lifestyle they've held onto for decades. The bonus lies in you to create a compelling business case to draw them in and, most importantly, deliver on your promises.

Chapter 5

Determining When and Where to Invest

By this point, you should know that Senior Living can be an excellent place to build a well-performing investment portfolio. According to expert real estate analysts, Senior Living investments have outpaced commercial real estate investment — and almost every other type of housing investment — for the past 10 to 15 years. Senior Living is a recession-proof, long-term real estate investment plan with low risk, high demand, and high returns.

But we are nothing if not thorough. Before diving into this market, we have a few secrets you should know that will ultimately help you build a more robust portfolio and make the most informed decision possible about where to invest, regardless of whether you are investing your own hard-earned cash, or pooling money from other investors in a joint venture, syndicate or fund.

Criteria for Senior Living Facilities

As any investor knows, the most important thing one can do when considering a sizable investment is to know exactly what they're getting themselves into. For someone like you who is considering Senior Living as an investment opportunity, it's imperative for you to consider which type of Senior Living facility you want to invest in. My partner and I have been developing Residential Assisted Living (RAL) and Memory Care (MC) properties for the most part.

Furthermore, choosing the right type of Senior Living facility depends on the elderly community the facility will serve while considering your personal investment needs. Senior requirements for care and facilities are varied and can change regularly. On the other hand, your investment needs will largely depend on how much you can invest and how involved you want to be in the process. We've listed some of the most common considerations below:

Home Maintenance and Personal Care Needs

Even if you invest in projects where the seniors will be living independently, you'll still want to keep their needs in mind. Even independent Senior Living homes will need regular cleaning and maintenance to ensure their living environment remains clean, comfortable, well-maintained, and safe. And seniors in those homes may need periodic assistance with personal care, including such things as offering cleaning services inside their individual units.

On the other hand, seniors who require more involved assistance, such as reminders to take medication, or those who cannot feed or bathe themselves, would benefit most from a RAL unit or an onsite caregiver.

Location Needs

As with all other aspects of any real estate project, your consideration for location needs will be two-fold, ensuring that you benefit from your investment and that the residents benefit from living in your Senior Living properties.

Rural facilities are the most popular for many seniors due to the natural serenity that comes with being away from city-oriented hustle and bustle. However, even the most rural locations must still be openly accessible.

When choosing a location for your project or scoping out already planned projects for your investment, consider how easy it is for visitors to come and go. Friends and family should be able to visit regularly, and the location should not hinder obtaining emergency services. Additionally, it should be in a location where internet and cell phone service are openly available. This will ensure the elderly do not feel isolated and allow you to easily check in on the project.

www.VinneyChopra.com/FreeBenefits

Keep in mind, though, that while investing in these types of facilities can yield big results, the success rate can vary based on several factors, including:

Location requirements – Senior Living homes are more expensive than regular housing units due to the additional amenities and facilities required to enrich the lives of the elderly. And while your first instinct may be to look at rural facilities, there are other location factors you should consider.

Locations with a high percentage of seniors are the most viable for investing, and those in areas with a higher population have a better chance of finding qualified staff. Regardless of whether you choose a metropolitan or rural location, however, your priority should be to ensure that your Senior Living location is safe, serene, and secure for its inhabitants. It should also be accessible for family members, staff, new arrivals, and current residents.

The economics of supply and demand – Supply and demand both play a huge role in the choice to invest. As we discussed previously, perhaps the strongest reason to buy any business is your potential ROI. In this case, your ROI will be highest if the location you select has a large aging population that is on the cusp of requiring a Senior Living facility.

Keep in mind that supply vs. demand numbers differ in every community. Currently, however, demand is outrunning supply in nearly every location, so regardless of where you choose, you are likely setting yourself up for success.

Amenities

While amenities can seem like nothing but extra expenses to the newbie investor, they represent opportunities to make your project soar. When choosing a new location to relocate a senior, families look at how easy it will be for their elderly loved ones to get around and what services will be provided to help them live relatively normal lives.

This includes things like elevators rather than flights of stairs, specially constructed or retrofitted washrooms, professional food preparation facilities, and common areas designed with the elderly in mind. It may also include space for event nights where the elderly can participate in social events such as Bingo, arts and crafts, etc.

When choosing your investment, you must take these things into account so that your project is at the ideal intersection of budget-friendly and elder-inclusive.

Financial Needs

Living alone can place a great financial burden on an aging person, whereas Senior Living homes, while expensive, represent better value. Because of this, you want to make sure your project cost doesn't cause consumer costs to be higher than what most people are willing to pay. If this does happen, you will create a dip in your project's demand that may well cause your pursuit to fail.

Consequently, when looking at what prices to set for elderly admission and maintenance, we recommend that you aim for something that will reduce the overall cost of living for the elderly. We'll explain a bit more about how to do this in other sections of this book.

Whether you are new to Senior Living investing or are looking to branch out your current portfolio, the opportunity offered here is not only ideal for today's elderly population but also offers financial security and a place for them (or you) to live out final years in comfort. Because of this, the investment you are making is not only one for your current self as an investor but also potentially for your own future self as a resident as well.

Many active investors have looked into their own futures and said, "Where will I go when I can no longer maintain my current home and/or live on my own?" Some have chosen to create future living quarters for themselves, as well as provide comfortable living quarters for other seniors in the community.

Conducting a Feasibility Study

Before investing your hard-earned money in any project, you want to have all relevant information at your disposal. Most active investors will conduct a feasibility study to help them make predictions about the future financial performance of the investment.

In simple terms, a feasibility study is an analysis that looks at all the possible angles a project can take on its journey to success (or failure). When doing a feasibility study, investors consider relevant factors, including economic, technical, legal, and scheduling considerations. A feasibility study should include a close look at demographic shifts and demand for Senior Living in a selected market.

Project managers, developers, buyers, and passive investors (collectively investors) typically rely on a feasibility study to weigh the advantages and disadvantages of developing and/or operating a project before they invest a lot of time and money into it. Similarly, financial institutions will typically demand an in-depth study of the market before financing a Senior Living project for a developer or buyer.

During the feasibility study, you will examine the income level of the target demographic to ensure you're not pricing your Senior Living units out of the market. A high-income target market means you can invest more in amenities and rent the units at a higher price point, leading to a higher ROI.

Feasibility studies will also help determine the competition in the area you're trying to invest in. Are there other Senior Living options in that area that offer better services, amenities, and rates?

You will typically hire a professional to prepare a feasibility study for you. Here is a granular breakdown of the components in a feasibility study that potential investors will want to examine:

Component #1: The Market

There are several types of Senior Living projects to invest in, including:

- Apartments for 55+
- Independent living
- Assisted living (specifically for senior citizens)
- Memory care
- Nursing homes

According to the experts, the most profitable and in-demand Senior Living projects are **independent living, assisted living, and memory care** homes for the elderly. With a comprehensive feasibility study, an investor will know where to direct their money, time, and energy.

Additionally, investors should make it a point to understand the merit of the study's sources. Data from trusted government agencies is preferred over data from third-party organizations that can manipulate the information they publish. A good rule of thumb is to obtain sources from a website ending in .gov. If a source has a website that doesn't end in .gov, however, that doesn't necessarily mean their data is unreliable. It simply indicates you should do further research into the merit of their data and reputation to determine their accuracy and reliability.

There are a few different statistics you should request in your feasibility study. Your data could include a demographic study of the state, communities, market trends, and shifts in demographics in your selected markets. In short, the feasibility study should fully review everything that could impact the investment, whether positively or negatively.

A feasibility study will do more than simply compile statistics, however. It should also make accurate conclusions from the information obtained.

Component #2: The Competition

The second most important component in your feasibility study will be a full-scale analysis of the competition.

This is an aspect many new investors either forgo or forget because of their inexperience. After all, it is easy to think to oneself, "As long as my business/investment functions the best and provides the best experience, competition does not matter."

This could not be more wrong.

Competition is a finicky thing that tells you nearly everything you need

to know about how to succeed. By analyzing the competition in your area, you can easily determine what is working for them and what is not, understand what needs improvement, and figure out if it is even possible to compete for a sizable market share there. Additionally, your competition will show you what the consumers in your area are looking for.

Let's look at an example:

Let's pretend that there are two Senior Living projects in your area, and you are considering introducing a third.

A detailed analysis of the first home shows that they are very industry-focused. They are equipped with above-average amenities, but their staff can be very impersonal. Because of this, there is a low resident satisfaction rating, and the resident turnover tends to be high.

In the second home, the staff is resident-focused. They connect well with the seniors living there, and the care is exceptional. However, the residents often find themselves bored due to the lack of amenities like walking tracks and game night events.

After analyzing these two competitors, one can reasonably determine that the consumers in this area are probably tired of having to choose between high-quality amenities and high-quality care. When you move into the area, focusing on combining these two things will almost ensure the success of your investment by filling a void in the local industry.

As you research your own area, your research team should analyze up to ten properties in that market area and draw competitive data such as costs, amenities, and access to medical care. Your team will also group the analyzed homes separately and identify what works for them, then draw up a strategy for you should you decide to compete in that market area.

Your research team should also determine the volume of need in that area versus the volume of establishments. If this ratio is too low and indicates there is little room for additional Senior Living units in that location, you may want to consider going somewhere else.

After all, this is finished, your research team should offer educated recommendations, including plans for better amenities, better access to medical services, a more effective method of reaching additional prospects, and a better marketing strategy to reach more prospective residents and their families in the desired area.

Component #3: Demand

As stated in the previous section, you will want to invest in Senior Living projects where the demand for such facilities is high, such as areas with a large population of Baby Boomers (55 years and older).

There are areas in the country where the demand for Senior Living housing is higher. For example, states such as California, Florida, and Georgia have a higher demand for Senior Living housing and a disproportionate number of elderly citizens. Investing in high-demand areas like these can boost your portfolio and earning potential, thereby maximizing your investment. While there may be high demand across the board, you ideally want to find the location where demand is highest.

To examine demand in various areas, your feasibility study should examine historical data from the past ten years as well as projected data for the next ten years. It should also investigate how the laws of your target state affect the demand for Senior Living to determine which areas are ultimately right for you.

Component #4: Age Of Property

The age of a property you're investing in plays a major role in the success of your investment.

As an investor, you want to place your money in a modern facility that offers the best technology available. You want to choose amenities and designs that will stand the test of time to minimize the effect of new competitors coming into your area 15 years down the road with Senior Living projects that could render yours obsolete. Alternatively, you can build in plans to renovate and improve your Senior Living project at specific intervals to keep it up to date.

Take Atlanta, GA, as an example. In this city, most senior housing is more than 15 years old. With new investors coming in, investors in older properties are at risk of losing out; a newer facility will always get more demand than an old one due to updated technologies and more modern designs.

The only way to survive in any market with an older building is to reduce pricing, upgrade your facilities, and improve your marketing message. As such, the feasibility study should analyze the age of an existing property and current competition to help direct your efforts. The research team will also determine other facilities in the area that could shift demand from your potential property to a newer one.

Additionally, the feasibility study should recommend whether there are other potential properties in the area or if a new build would be your best course of action.

Component #5: Income Level

To succeed, your research team should investigate the income level of the area and age group you're trying to target; the higher the income, the more your residents will spend. Your feasibility study should include research on the income level of your target age group and advise how best to proceed.

It is advisable for investors to seek opportunities with higher income. While the Senior Living market is low risk, investing in high-income areas makes that risk even smaller, as higher-income families are more likely to be able to afford the cost of private senior housing.

Unless you have very deep pockets and can assume the risks involved with investing in lower-income areas, it's wise to stick to higher-income demographics. However, if you *are* someone who wants to invest in a lower-income area, we'll be covering more on that later in this book. You may have to conduct feasibility studies for several different areas or investment opportunities to determine which of them is right for you. Once you utilize those studies to finalize your location, though, you're ready to start investing!

Chapter 6

Financing a Senior Living Project

Financing Options for Senior Living Property

Mortgage: One of the easiest ways to get your foot in the door as a passive Senior Living investor is to use a mortgaged loan to purchase the commercial property on which a facility can be built. Then, you rent it to the Senior Living owner and use part of your monthly proceeds to pay off the mortgage.

Private Loan: Purchasing the property on a private sector loan: Contrary to a typical bank loan, private sector loans are given to investors like you by individuals looking to do their own passive investing. The terms can often be more favorable than bank loans due to the more personal nature of the transaction.

Private Capital: You can raise capital for your Senior Living investments from passive investors who think your Senior Living facility is a worthy venture. There are securities laws that must be followed if you are going to raise capital from passive investors, so you will need to learn how to legally raise private money if you are going to go this route. This is called "syndication." More about this later...

Joint Venture: This refers to individuals and entities who are actively involved in acquiring, owning, and operating the facility with you, usually in a legal entity such as a member-managed limited liability company. Investors who contribute money must be actively involved in generating their own profit for your operation to be considered a joint venture that is not subject to compliance with securities laws. This can work if there are only 1-5 members but doesn't work well for groups larger than that. If you will have more than 4-5 investors, it will be better for you to syndicate and raise capital from passive investors.

Loans

A mortgage or private loan, as described above, involves borrowing money from third parties. This allows you to "leverage" the investment and generate a higher ROI for yourself and others.

Here's how this works: Lenders typically want less interest than private investors want. Therefore, if you can finance a portion of the project with a bank loan, you will increase the amount left over after paying the loan payments (i.e., debt service) that can be shared between your investors and you.

Typically, lending money involves the borrower signing a promissory note, in effect, a financial 'IOU' that is legally binding, and that names the property and our business as collateral for the loan. This means that if you don't make the required payments and pay the loan back as agreed, the lender can foreclose and take over ownership of the property and/or your Senior Living business. In this case, all that you (and/or your investors) have invested in the property or business could be lost.

The promissory note means that you are promising to pay the lender the money you owe them. The lender is entitled to receive a specific amount at specific intervals, usually monthly, plus a rate of interest on their money and an eventual return of principal. In most traditional loans, banks are the holders of a promissory note. They lend out money to real estate investors and/or small business owners like you, and you, as the borrower, signs a series of loan papers.

Before lending to your Senior Living business, the lender may want to obtain personal guarantees from the members of your management team. In this case, you will have to prove that your management team has a collective net worth equal to or greater than the loan amount. If you don't have this on your own, you will need to admit other people into your management team who can provide this net worth. This could be a condition of obtaining a loan.

Most investors in the Senior Living space opt to obtain a bank loan if one is available. If you are considering this course of action, you should know that a bank won't give you a penny unless they see a well-structured, viable business plan that is all but guaranteed to bring in sufficient revenue to cover your loan and interest payments, plus a qualified and experienced operator, and loan guarantors with sufficient net worth. You should create a business proposal that clearly communicates your plan for your Senior Living project to both prospective lenders and to your prospective investors.

Syndication: A New Perspective on Raising Capital

Raising capital for Senior Living projects is another topic of discussion. Some investors are ready to invest in this niche because they see it producing positive outcomes across the country, but they don't want to be involved daily. Not all investors are interested in owning and operating Senior Living homes. Some of them just want to invest in real estate. Your job is to educate investors on why Senior Living investing makes sense so they can decide whether to invest with you on future projects.

How Syndication Works

Syndication is a process of pooling money from other people (with minimal investment from you) to purchase an asset that no single investor could acquire individually.

It is paramount to find like-minded people to invest in your 'syndicate' with. A syndicate, in this context, is simply a group of investors, some active and some passive, that has been formed to acquire or develop, own, and operate a specific property. The challenge is to find a property that will generate an annualized ROI from a combination of cash flow profits and resale profits (leftover after paying operating expenses and bank loan obligations and repaying the capital contributions of all investors).

SEC Rules

When you are using funds contributed by private investors, there are specific rules governed by the United States Securities and Exchange Commission (SEC) that must be followed. You must learn the rules or risk a regulatory investigation and enforcement action and being forced to give your investors' money back. An excellent resource for this is Attorney Kim Lisa Taylor's book: "How to Raise Capital for Real Estate *Legally*," available on Amazon. Her book contains a section on how to structure a Residential Assisted Living project with investors, as well as explaining SEC rules on raising private money.

Participants in a Syndicate

In a syndicate, there are two components:

- The *syndicator* (also known as the *sponsor*). These are people, like my business partner and I, who play an active role in the process of finding a suitable property, conducting feasibility studies, and who develop or acquire Senior Living properties. The syndicators act as "asset managers" who oversee operations at the Senior Living facility on behalf of their passive investors. Often, the syndicator's own money is not invested, but they do put in active effort and time by acquiring and/or developing the property, overseeing the onsite operations manager, and the eventual sale of the facility.
- Passive *investors*. Investors contribute the cash needed to acquire and set up the property, plus closing costs, reserves, and certain fees earned by the syndicator. They observe a passive role in the syndication process. They provide the money

but don't engage in the daily running of the facility and have limited voting rights.

Important Considerations When Syndicating

When setting up a syndicate, it's important to consider several factors for the proposed facility, including:

- The team members who will be actively involved in raising capital, guaranteeing bank loans, getting the facility ready for occupancy, hiring staff, and overseeing on-site operations; this is your syndication management team.
- The feasibility study and its conclusions and recommendations.
- The projected profitability of the proposed facility.

Building Your Syndication Team

Your basic syndication team members should be composed of the following specialists:

- Your finance team includes your mortgage broker, loan guarantors, and members of your syndication management team who will help raise capital from investors.
- Passive Investors who share your passion, not only for the investment; but for providing safe and comfortable Senior Living housing.
- A real estate attorney to help close the real estate transaction
- A corporate securities attorney who will prepare your securities offering documents so you can legally raise money from private investors.
- Your Senior Living operator or management company (if you plan to hire one) or the staff members you will hire if you will be managing the facility on your own. You want to make sure that your management team or staff consists of people who are

invested in caring for the elderly and ensuring they have the best quality of life in your facility.

Positivity breeds creative thinking. Setting and reaching your professional goals is essential for personal happiness and professional success, but you can't do it alone. Bringing people into your investment strategy who are equally enthusiastic will ultimately bring the long-term success you desire.

How To Build An Investor Database

To build up a passive investor base, you'll need to take the following steps:

Step 1: Invest In Your Education

Everyone knows that careful preparation prevents poor performance.

The importance of education in any business venture cannot be overemphasized. Having intrinsic knowledge of your industry or business prevents unnecessary mistakes and helps you make well-informed decisions. Luckily, by reading this book, you have already begun the long path toward establishing your education in both the real estate sector and as a Senior Living expert.

Now, if you're thinking seriously about actively investing in Senior Living, or organizing your own group of passive investors to do so, here's what you'll need to know:

Discover and Learn

Discover and learn as much about this business as you can. Invest in your knowledge about Senior Living before pledging your time and money to this business. This requires conducting personal market research to identify areas like:

- Senior population growth reports
- Already built Senior Living properties

www.VinneyChopra.com/FreeBenefits

- Appealing environments, lakes, golf courses, and a serene atmosphere
- Local economy reports, demographic net worth and affordability, and trends
- State and County codes and requirements, certificates, and compliance issues

An excellent way to gain knowledge of this industry is to volunteer at a Senior Living home near you for anywhere from a few weeks to a few months. In doing this, you will expose yourself to the industry in a way many of your competitors won't have. You'll hear the complaints of the residents, talk in person with the families, and better understand how to keep your employees satisfied. To be honest, volunteering at a Senior Living facility will give you an edge on the competition that will shine through in every decision you make.

Doing this will also give you the opportunity to do your due diligence. In any business venture, you need to do your homework. Exposing yourself to the daily grind of your industry helps you do this by teaching you to understand:

- Where crises occur and take the necessary precautions.
- How employees feel and how they interact with seniors in the facilities.
- How the facilities and amenities affect the lives of seniors who live there.

Get a Mentor

Having a mentor can also help. A mentor can help guide your journey into actively investing in Senior Living projects. The input of a mentor that has experience in Senior Living makes all the difference and can help you navigate your way around investing in Senior Living while preventing you from making costly mistakes with yours or other people's money.

There are various ways to approach a mentor to gain investment experience.

The relationship could be transactional, where you pay them for their time in exchange for their advice and expertise (much like a consultant).

If permitted, you could shadow your mentor or intern at their place of business to gain valuable insight, education, and experience. We find this method to be a highly effective way to proactively add value while you gain expertise that you can apply to future ventures.

To find a person willing to mentor you, consider joining Facebook groups or Reddit boards dedicated to this form of investment.

Step 2: Talk The Talk

Every industry has insider terminology, specific phrases, and verbiage common to professionals in that field. Using common industry language will give you confidence and will also help you be perceived as an expert in the field. When you don't use the insider lingo, however, it is usually glaringly obvious to seasoned investors that you are a beginner and may be inexperienced. This could negatively affect your ability to gain traction amongst investors.

An effective way of dealing with this issue is to familiarize yourself with the terminology used by professional Senior Living investors and real estate investors in general. The next chapter contains some basic underwriting terms and guidelines to help get you started.

Step 3: Build Your Brand

You will need to take steps to build your brand as you establish your Senior Living investment business. Here are a few pointers that will help your brand stand out from the crowd:

Research your target audience: You must be attuned to the needs of both your investors and your residents. Learn what they want and know how to give it to them. You'll eventually need a marketing plan for both.

First impressions matter: Your brand is how people perceive you, consciously and unconsciously; your brand represents *you*. It is the first step toward the decision-making process, where an investor will decide whether to invest with you or where a resident will decide to live in your Senior Living project.

Basic requirements: When approaching investors and prospective residents for your Senior Living project, there are basic considerations that determine the long-term viability of your Senior Living business and facilities. You'll need to consider each of these factors and portray them in the best light to attract investors and residents.

Basic considerations your brand might highlight could include such things as:

- What category of Senior Living establishments do you plan to provide?
- Is there a common name you will use for all of your facilities?
- How will you screen and train your staff?
- What are the demographic criteria for areas you plan to invest in?
- Planned accreditation of facilities, operators, or staff
- How do you determine resident pricing?
- What is your projected net profit, and how is it determined?

Step 4: Share Your Passion for Senior Living With Your Investors

People invest in ventures they find worthwhile and highly profitable, but they also invest in passionate people whom they believe can make that happen.

When attracting investors, you must convince them that a partnership with *you* is the right decision. Potential investors will evaluate you and what you're selling. By now, we know that Senior Living investment is highly lucrative, but to attract investors, you'll need to sell *them* on the investment opportunity. That's why it's important to emphasize the benefits of your venture by arming yourself with facts and statistics. A highly successful investment or business venture is always based on careful projections and deliberate decisions supported by facts and experience.

Luckily, there is a wealth of statistics that indicate Senior Living investment is a high-yield/low-risk endeavor. Here are some examples:

- According to the World Health Organization (WHO), the proportion of the world's population over 60 years old will nearly double from 12% to 22% between 2015-2050.
- By 2020, the number of people aged 60 and older will outnumber children younger than five years old.
- American commercial real estate services and investment firm Coldwell Banker Richard Ellis (CBRE) released the *US Seniors Housing and Care Investors, Survey and Trends Report*, which provides data indicating that 19% of surveyed business operators already have some type of investment in this sector. Meanwhile, another 20% indicated their interest in investing in the future.

Step 5: Build Relationships With Your Potential Investors

No one likes to feel like they're being used. And if you find an investor and get straight to the facts and numbers of why they should invest with you, that's exactly how they're going to feel.

A successful business is built on relationships, which is a complex and highly essential art form. A major prerequisite to effective relationship building is to engage investors before you need their money. Investors choose their projects for two major reasons; because of the potential for profit, or as the result of previously established relationships. To build your relationship with investors, it is important to think less as a 'founder' and more as a 'marketer.'

Develop Relationships With Investors Before Asking Them To Invest

Start by making a list of everyone you know, including family members and friends, members of civic organizations you belong to, and your prior resident base. The SEC requires that you have a "pre-existing, substantive relationship" with each prospective investor before you invite them to invest in your projects (i.e., make "offers").

The "substantive relationship" means you have to have "suitability" conversations with each prospective investor to determine whether their goals are in line with yours and whether they might be suitable investors for your Senior Living projects. This suitability conversation must take place before you start making them offers to invest – that's what is meant by a "pre-existing relationship."

The suitability conversation includes asking each prospective investor if they are accredited or sophisticated. Accredited investors must have over $1 Million in net worth, excluding equity in their primary residence, or they must make over $200,000/year if single or $300,000/year if married. Sophisticated investors may have other real estate investments, operate small businesses, or have other investment experience that makes them capable of understanding the merits and risks of an investment in a Senior Living project that you might offer them in the future. To be sophisticated, an investor must have more than just some savings and a job.

Document what you learned during the suitability conversation, as it's an SEC requirement, and you may need this documentation later to prove that you followed the SEC's rules for private investment offerings and that you did, in fact, have a pre-existing substantive relationship in place with every investor before offering them the ability to invest with you.

The above requirements are part of a securities exemption called Regulation D, Rule 506(b), regulated by the SEC. This rule allows you to raise an unlimited amount of money from an unlimited number of accredited investors and up to 35 non-accredited but sophisticated investors, *but you can't find them through any means of general advertising or solicitation*. The way to prove you didn't advertise is to be able to demonstrate that you had the pre-existing, substantive relationship described above. This is the friends, family, and acquaintances exemption.

There is another exemption, Regulation D, Rule 506(c), that allows you to advertise but restricts you to only including verified accredited investors. You won't be successful advertising until you have done a series of successful Rule 506(b) offerings with your family, friends, and acquaintances, so plan on developing pre-existing, substantive relationships with investors before you ask them to invest. Even if you were allowed to advertise, it's a really good idea to get to know investors before you invite them into your offering, as the wrong investors can make your life difficult.

Where To Meet New Investors

There are a wide variety of places where informal and personal introductions can be made in a social environment, from corporate events, and social meetups to country clubs. No matter where you choose to rally potential investors, the decorum for fostering good working relationships is the same:

- **Put yourself out there!** Ask for an introduction; meet investors at local clubs, and social or volunteer events; seek investors out on specific online platforms; or simply send an email or call people you know and tell them what you're doing. You will not be successful in raising capital if you lock yourself in your basement.
- **Follow up regularly**, but make sure you're not inundating potential investors with useless information just to "stay in

touch." Filling someone's inbox with irrelevant content will make you look desperate.

- **Be patient.** Relationships take time, patience, diligence, and hard work. Always keep your goals in mind but invest the time into making these relationships authentic.

Build Your Elevator Pitch

You should know your business inside and out and be able to deliver it to a potential investor in 30 seconds or less. You never know where your next opportunity lies, so you should always be ready to talk about what you do, who you do it for, and how it benefits investors when the opportunity presents itself.

Brace for rejection

Not all investors will like your ideas. Rejection is an opportunity to step back, reflect and re-strategize so that you'll be better prepared the next time.

Be A Professional

While you strive to improve your networking skills and build your pool of investors, be calm, gathered, and prepared to answer questions. Be assertive, not aggressive, and try not to sound desperate, which can send potential investors running away from you and towards another opportunity.

Step 6: Keep In Contact

The most important building block to creating an effective team is staying in contact. To strengthen the team bond, you need to keep the lines of communication open and keep all your investors well-informed. Never hesitate to display your passion and mission. It has been verified that investors continually seek passionate and tenacious founders. Communicating your action plans and goals will go a long way to increasing their confidence in you as a highly competent leader with a vision.

Here are some simple methods to keep your investors in the loop:

Emails and newsletters are easy and effective tools you can leverage to disseminate information about your company to your investors. General company newsletters on what your branded entity is doing (across all projects) can offer insights into company news and updates, reports, and press releases and can be sent quarterly. The content of your newsletters could be a mix of educational, informative, and promotional content. They may also contain announcements, links to important and related journals and events.

Emails can be sent on a more regular cadence for things that require urgent attention or for project-specific information you need to convey to that project's investors. A well-detailed status update email could contain:

- Notable milestones at the Senior Living project.
- Updates on how investor money is being spent.
- An alert on any issue or crisis you might be facing.
- Quarterly financial and project reports showing key metrics for the project; occupancy rates, status of improvement projects, status of marketing campaigns, cash in the bank, monthly cash flow and expenses, staff highlights and awards, notable senior stories, etc.
- Annual reports, such as tax documents.

Meetings. Organize quarterly investor meetings where important project status updates can be discussed. Your relationship with investors should be continuous — they are just as invested in your company's success as you are, and they may want to know about other investment opportunities for themselves or for their friends! They are your allies; as such, it is essential that you are proactive in building a strong and harmonious investor relationship. A good meeting should be highly engaging, informative and cover a breadth of topics such as:

- Cash flow.
- Key development and changes.
- Important and encouraging projects completed.
- Events that facilitate bonding and effective communication among staff and/or residents.

Phone calls are increasingly undervalued in today's digital age, yet they're still the fastest way to communicate immediate information. Calls can be a means of keeping in contact when important and urgent decisions must be made, a challenge arises, when a major change has been made, or when additional funds are needed.

Chapter 7

Analyzing Profitability for a Senior Living Project

Before you can syndicate, you have to determine whether your Senior Living facility will generate sufficient income return to pay all of the property operating expenses, any loan payments, your staff salaries, your investors, and you!

Investing Terminology

First, let's discuss some basic terms you need to understand as you analyze your projects:

- **Average Annualized Return:** This is calculated by adding cash flow returns paid (or projected) to all investors (active and passive) plus equity generated on sale, divided by the number of years the cash was invested, and then dividing the result by the amount of cash invested in a project (excluding debt).
- **Cash Flow**: It's very important to look at the profit and loss statements for a Senior Living facility (P&Ls) or create them for development projects in order to make projections as to whether investors (or you) will be able to get a good return on investment. I cover this in more detail in my 1st book on Amazon, Apartment Syndication Made Easy - A Step-by-Step Guide to Investing in Commercial Real Estate, which you can buy here.
- **Debt service:** The monthly mortgage payment (interest and/or principal) on loans taken out against the property and/or the business.
- **Debt service coverage ratio (DSCR)**: A ratio depicting the money required to cover the repayment of interest and principal on a debt for a particular period divided by the Net Operating Income (NOI) generated by the property.

- **Internal rate of return (IRR):** The annual rate of growth an investment is expected to generate, taking into account the original cash investment plus the time value of money.
- **Loan to cost (LTC) vs. loan to value (LTV):** LTC compares the loan amount for a real estate project against the amount needed to acquire or develop the project. LTV compares the loan amount to the expected market value of a completed project.
- **Net Operating Income (NOI):** Net operating income (NOI) is a calculation used to analyze the profitability of income-generating real estate investments. NOI equals all revenue from the property minus all reasonably necessary operating expenses, excluding debt service. NOI is a before-tax figure appearing on a property's income and cash flow statement that excludes principal and interest payments on loans, capital expenditures, depreciation, and amortization. When this metric is used in other industries, it is referred to as "EBIT," which stands for "earnings before interest and taxes."
- **Net Present Value (NPV):** The difference between the present value of cash inflows and the present value of cash outflows over a period of time. NPV is used in investment planning to determine the profitability of your project.
- **Occupancy rate:** The ratio of rented or used space to the total amount of available space. For senior housing, the rate is usually determined by dividing the number of occupied beds by the number of beds a facility has.
- **Return on Investment (ROI):** A return on investment (ROI) measures how much profit is made from an investment compared to the cash invested.

Chapter 8

Splitting Cash With Passive Investors in a Senior Living Project

Mastering the Art of Syndicate Cash Split: A Comprehensive Guide

The dynamics of syndicate or fund management and cash flow splitting is a complex puzzle. However, it is a puzzle that can be solved with an astute comprehension of financial metrics and the right guidance. Here I will attempt to give the ideas from my 16 years of learning this business. Actually, I authored my first book, "Apartment Syndication Made Easy – A Step-by-Step Guide.

Real Estate Investment: Numbers Speak Volumes

Real estate investment has always been a game of numbers, with strategies based on cash flow, sales proceeds, equity gains, and investor returns. If the "annualized cash on cash" return of a property fails to hover around 10-15%, it might be time to reconsider. There are a few real estate analyses and Commercial Underwriter software available to make the calculations clearer and easier.

The Rise and Fall of Target Annualized Cash on Cash Return

Investor returns fluctuate as per changing market conditions such as interest rates and property demand. The target annualized cash-on-cash return has ranged from low to mid-20s in past years, while it has been in the mid to high teens in recent times.

Steps to Calculate Your Syndicate's Cash Flow and Investor Split

Step 1: Estimation of Funds Needed

Your property acquisition costs come first. If a $4M property is purchased with a 75% loan to value ratio, you'll need $1M for the down payment and additional costs for capital improvements, legal fees, lender fees, and more. As a rule of thumb, estimate about 1/3 of the purchase price as your raise amount for a value-add project.

Step 2: Determining Annual Cash-on-Cash Return from Cash Flow

A detailed pro forma projection will help you to calculate the annual cash-on-cash return that your property will generate on your investment over your expected ownership period. Here, the "net operating income" and "distributable cash" play crucial roles.

Step 3: Calculating Cash-on-Cash Return from Sale

By modeling a proposed exit strategy, you can calculate your projected sale price and the distributable cash from the sale. The formula $V = I/R$, where R equals the capitalization rate; I equals net operating income, and V equals the estimated sale price, will be used here.

Step 4: Evaluating Annualized Cash-on-Cash Returns

Add up all the distributable cash paid to stakeholders during the deal's lifetime. Divide this total by the years you've held the property to obtain your annualized cash-on-cash return. The property's overall cash-on-cash return should ideally be 20% or more.

Step 5: Working Out Your Split with Investors

Here, you determine your split by dividing the target return for investors by the property's total annualized cash-on-cash return. For instance, if you want to offer a 15% return to investors and your property's return is 20%, investors should receive 75% of the deal. This calculates to a 75/25 split between investors (Class A) and management (Class B).

The Art of Splitting Management Earnings

The management of a syndicate or fund demands careful allocation of manager's fees and Class B (profit) distributions. Typically, the same percentage of ownership interest in a fund will mirror the member's percentage of Class B interests.

However, a disproportionately larger share of certain managers' fees can be allocated based on specific tasks performed. For instance, the asset manager could share some Class B interests with those providing services but not participating in management decisions or loan guarantees.

The allocation of asset management percentage interests is generally divided into four sections:

1. **Pre-closing activities (25%)**: This includes property discovery, due diligence, loan coordination, and corporate structure organization.
2. **Property operations oversight (25%)**: This involves regular meetings with property managers and contractors, overseeing accounting, and tax filings.
3. **Loan guarantors (20-25%)**: Non-recourse loans require members of the asset management entity with a collective net worth equal to or more than the loan amount.
4. **Investor relations (25-30%)**: This category includes fundraising and managing investor relations.

In conclusion, understanding how to split cash in a syndicate or fund requires careful calculation, an understanding of the market dynamics, and an ability to forecast returns. Armed with this knowledge, you can make informed decisions that will benefit both you and your investors.

CASH DISTRIBUTIONS & WATERFALLS

Member distributions will be clearly specified in the offering documents prepared by your corporate securities attorney. Management will evaluate, typically quarterly during property operations, whether there is distributable cash to disburse to the members.

Each phase of the syndicate's operation (cash flow, refinance, or sale) may have a separate distribution schedule, known as a "distribution waterfall." The waterfall outlines the sequence in which cash is distributed during each phase until all of it has been disbursed.

Simple waterfalls are effective, whereas complicated ones are not. I have come across documents with 10-12 steps in the distribution waterfall that nobody could comprehend. When investors fail to understand, they simply choose not to invest.

Pari Passu vs. Pro Rata Distributions

Your company will typically distribute cash to investors either pro rata or pari passu. Pro rata distributions mean they are allocated based on each investor's percentage interests. Pari passu generally means distributions will be made according to priority.

For instance, certain classes may receive distributions first (pari passu), but those distributions will then be further allocated among class members based on their percentage interests within that class (pro rata).

Making Cash Distributions

Distributions From Cash Flow

Option 1: During the property's ownership period, a typical syndicate may offer investors a straight split of distributable cash between the investors and the asset manager, usually on a pari passu basis (by class), and then pro rata (within each class).

Option 2: An alternative structure (and perhaps more common) is to offer a cumulative "preferred return" (typically 6% to 8%) to investors from cash flow. Preferred returns are calculated against the amount of the investor's capital contributions, with any remaining distributable cash split between the management class and investors.

Option 3: The real question is whether the management class should take a catchup distribution. We will explore all three of these options in this chapter.

Distributions From a Capital Transaction

When a capital transaction occurs, such as a refinance or sale, cash proceeds will be distributed in an order designed to pay back member capital contributions first and then make up arrearages in preferred returns, finally splitting the remaining cash between investors and management.

Example Distribution Waterfalls

In each scenario below, we will perform an "Analysis" to illustrate the numerical implications, using the following assumptions:

• Class A contributed $10M • The property generated $1M/year from cash flow ($5M total) • The property generated $5M of additional distributable cash on sale (after paying all closing expenses, loans, and returning capital to investors). • Adding this all together, the property generated a total return of $10M over 5 years; equaling an annualized cash-on-cash return of $2M/year • A $2M annualized return /$10M total capital contributions = a 20% overall annualized cash on cash return. • The descriptions below show a 70/30 split. If the returns aren't sufficient to entice investors (the target is mid to high teens); try changing the split and adjusting the numbers to a 75/25 split.

Table Illustrating the Waterfall Models Described Below

If you prefer a summarized comparison of the three waterfall models discussed in this chapter, illustrating how each model affects distributable cash for investors and the asset management team, please visit my very good friend and a top SEC attorney, Kim Lisa Taylor website:

https://RaiseCapitalForRealEstate.com/BookBonus.

Straight Split Scenario

The following waterfall represents a 70/30 split in a two-class company, also known as a straight split.

Distributions From Operations (Cash Flow)

Cash generated from property operations (cash flow) will be disbursed in the following order until exhausted:

• Distributable cash will be split between all members, with 70% allocated to Class A and 30% allocated to Class B members.

Analysis

In the straight split scenario, from cash flow:

1. Class A would receive 70% of $1M, or $700k/year from cash flow, and
2. Class B would receive 30%, or $300k/year.

Distributions From Capital Transactions

On refinance or sale of the property or dissolution of the company (after payment of expenses and liabilities), cash will be disbursed in the following order until exhausted:

• First, the Class A members will receive all of the distributable cash as a return of capital until they have received a refund of 100% of their unreturned capital contributions; • Second, any remaining distributable cash will be split 70/30 between all members, with 70% allocated to Class A and 30% allocated to Class B members.

Analysis

In the straight split scenario, on sale:

1. Class A would receive 70% of $5M, or $3.5M, and
2. Class B would receive 30% of $5M, or $1.5M.

What was Class A's cash on cash return? Class A received distributions of $700k/year for 5 years ($3.5M) plus $3.5M from the sale, for a total of $7M. Thus, Class A earned an overall return of 70%; when divided by the 5-year hold period, this equals a 14% annualized return on investment.

What was Class B's total return in numbers? Class B received $300k/year for 5 years ($1.5M), plus $1.5M on the sale, totaling $3M. Divided over 5 years, that was an annualized distribution of $600k.

Preferred Return With a 70/30 Split

The following waterfall reflects a 70/30 split, after payment of an 8% preferred return to Class A.

Distributions From Operations (Cash Flow)

Cash generated from property operations (cash flow) will be disbursed in the following order until exhausted:

• First, Class A members will be paid all of the distributable cash until they have received a non-compounded, cumulative annualized return of 8% (the preferred return), determined quarterly and calculated against the Class A unreturned capital contributions. • Second, any remaining distributable cash will be split 70/30 between the members, with 70% paid to Class A and 30% paid to Class B members.

Analysis

In the preferred return scenario, from cash flow:

1. Class A would receive an annual return of $800,000 ($200,000/quarter); plus.

2. Class A would also receive 70% of the remaining $200,000, or $140,000 (for a total of $940,000/year); and

3. Class B would receive 30% of the remaining $200,000, or $60,000/year.

Any arrearages (deficiencies) in Class A preferred returns will be deferred and made up from future cash flow or proceeds from a capital transaction, at the asset manager's option. There is no catchup for Class B, so whatever they get in any given year is all they ever get.

Distributions From Capital Transactions

On refinance or sale of the property or dissolution of the company (after payment of expenses and liabilities), cash will be disbursed in the following order until exhausted:

• First, to repay the unreturned capital contributions of Class A members; • Then, to make up arrearages in Class A preferred returns; • Any remaining cash will be split 70/30 between Class A and Class B.

Analysis

In the preferred return scenario, on sale:

1. As there are no deficiencies in our example, with respect to Class A preferred returns, as soon as Class A's unreturned capital contributions were repaid, the next step in the waterfall would be to make up deficiencies in Class B's catchup distributions. In this case, Class B would get $143,000 as a catchup for every year it was deficient. Assuming it was deficient every year for 5 years, Class B would be entitled to a catchup distribution of $143k/year ($143k x 5 years = $715k).

2. The remaining distributable cash would be split 70/30 between Class A and Class B. $5M minus $715k (arrearages paid to Class B) = $4,285,000. Class A would receive $2,999,500 (70%), and Class B would receive $1,285,500 (30%).

What was Class A's cash on cash return? Class A received distributions of $800k/year for 5 years ($4M) plus $2,999,500 from the sale for a total of $6,999,500. Thus, Class A earned an overall return of 69.99% ($6,999,500 ÷ $10M = 0.7; 0.7 x 100 = 69.99%). Class A's annualized return was 69.00% ÷ 5 years = 13.99%.

What was Class B's total return in numbers? Class B received $343k/year for 5 years for a total of $1,715,000 plus $1,285,500 on the sale, equaling total distributions of $3M. Divided over 5 years, that was an annualized distribution of $600k.

Final Word on Class B Catchups

As you can see, without the Class B catchup, you run the risk of paying all of the cash flow to investors both from property operations and from a capital transaction, leaving little (or none) to distribute to your asset management team. Further, you may even be creating a disconnect between your interests and those of your investors. For instance, if your investors are receiving cash flow from property operations but you aren't, they may want to keep the property long-term. However, because you aren't making any money for all of the work you are doing, the asset management team may have the incentive to sell the property so you can get paid from your share of the equity realized on sale. Or alternatively, you may have to keep chasing acquisition fees from other deals to support your own financial needs, turning your attention away from this property to the detriment of your investors.

The best way to ensure that you and your investors' interests are aligned is to create a waterfall scenario where both you, as the asset manager, and your investors make money from all phases of property ownership.

I trust this explanation will help you understand the importance of this concept. I realize that not all deals will support this structure, but they should always be considered when underwriting your deals.

The scenario I presented above may be more optimistic than what you will encounter in real life. You are much more likely to find deals that don't have 8% returns in the first 2-3 years, leaving deficiencies in Class A returns that must be made up on sale, further diminishing the amounts available for distribution to Class B. This typically results in no distributions to Class B for the first 2-3 years, and without a Class B catchup, you will never be able to make up Class B distributions for those years.

Consider these models when you are doing your underwriting, and, if the property can support it, include the Class B catchups to protect yourselves and the members of the asset management entity. The asset manager can always elect to forego any management fee or any distribution to which Class B is entitled if you wish to achieve your projected returns for Class A. It's better to give yourself the ability to collect the Class B catchup if you have sufficient funds than to give away all of the proceeds to Class A and be sorry you didn't protect yourself. Most of our clients only make this mistake one time.

Variations to Consider

Change the Split to Match the Target Returns for Investors

The returns shown in the example waterfalls above (and in the bonus table) are based on a 70/30 split. The target for investors is an annualized return in the mid to high teens. If the returns based on a 70/30 split aren't sufficient to entice investors, try changing the split and adjusting the numbers to something like a 75/25 split.

Offer Lower Preferred Returns Until Stabilization

I once asked a representative from a large multi-family syndication company that has billions in assets under management whether they do

8% preferred returns, and their response was, "We don't offer 8% returns in the first 2-3 years, during the stabilization process. During that time, we offer 5 or 6% returns, and then go to 8% after stabilization and refinance." Something for you to consider. That way you don't have to go back and make up arrearages.

Limit Preferred Returns to the First 1-2 Years

Another option is to consider a preferred return that only lasts for 1 or 2 years; after which it goes to a straight split.

Place Caps on Investor Returns

Another common option is to cap investor returns such that once all of Class A's capital contributions have been repaid and they have received an annualized return of a pre-determined percentage, such as 18%, the split changes to 50/50 or even flips, so that from then on, it's 30/70.

A Word on Buying Out Investors on Refinance

Investors don't like this. Clients have tried this in the past and come back to tell us investors hated it and wouldn't invest with them again. It's better to cap investor returns, change the split, and leave them in the deal, then it is to cash them out on refinance while you get the windfall of owning the property that your syndicate or fund bought with their money.

Partial Payback of Investors on Refinance

When you do a cash-out refinance, you should always use the proceeds to return investor capital contributions. The very nature of a refinance results in higher leverage on the property, and if prices drop (due to interest rate increases, oversupply, lack of financing, etc.), you could be left short when it comes to paying back investor capital contributions on sale. Additionally, if there is a preferred return for investors, from that point forward, you only owe it on their "unreturned capital contributions."

For example, it's common for a syndicate or fund to pay back 50% of investor capital from a property refinance. From that point forward, you would only owe investors a preferred return on the 50% of their original capital contributions that remain invested, leaving more cash available to split between Class A and Class B; that is, more for the asset manager.

Forever-Hold Models

In the typical waterfall models described above, you would typically count all cash flow returns as a return on investment and returns from capital transactions are usually always classified as a return of capital.

If you want to have a forever-hold model, then you may need to classify all cash flow distributions as a return of capital until all capital contributions are repaid, after which any further returns are classified as a return on investment. The nice thing about this model for investors is that they don't get taxed on returned capital, but they also don't get their capital contributions back in chunks that they can then reinvest. The best way to find out if your investors will like this model is to ask them if this model would work for them.

Distribution Models That Are Dangerous for Asset Managers

Kim Lisa Taylor writes, "I have reviewed many offering documents drafted by other attorneys, and I commonly see several scenarios that I believe are dangerous for asset managers":

1. The first is to pay arrearages in preferred returns before returning capital contributions. I always tell my clients, remove your liabilities first. You won't get sued for not making your preferred returns, but you will get sued if you don't return

capital. Pay back capital contributions first, and then make up arrearages in preferred returns.

2. The second is a model that some crowdfunding platforms and broker-dealers tend to favor. This scenario requires that you pay back all of the investors' capital contributions plus their preferred returns before the asset manager can collect any distributions at all. This means you could be operating a property for 5 or more years and trying to live off asset management fees, with no distributions to the management class until the sale. In my opinion, this misaligns your interests with investors. You can't wait to sell the property so that you can earn distributions from the sale, but investors are happily enjoying their cash flow returns, all while the asset management team starves. You may eventually have to turn your attention to paying deals or getting a job to survive, leaving their investment to suffer. Any waterfall that doesn't pay the asset manager along the way, or at least within a couple of years (and more than just asset management fees), is a recipe for a languishing investment. Investors shouldn't want this, and you shouldn't offer it. It's your job to educate them as to why it's in their best interests for you to earn distributions during ownership – and not just on sale.

3. A third model that often fails is trying to tailor your returns to individual investors – this is a rookie mistake; just don't do it. These are take-it-or-leave-it offerings. You've done the due diligence and the analysis; you know what will work for the long-term and for all investors, Don't let a few bullish investors try to influence you or make you carve out special deals for them – unless they are bringing in a significant amount of money that you can't raise any other way; or if they want to provide an additional service, such as co-guaranteeing a loan, or introducing you to all of their wealthy friends.

4. A fourth model I have seen gives asset managers carte blanche abilities to unilaterally change the terms of an offering and power of attorney over every investor to force them to go along. This is a dangerous position for investors because there is nothing to stop a bad asset manager from completely changing the terms of the deal to which investors originally agreed. Investors should beware of offerings that have such provisions, and you shouldn't give yourself that much power. This too is a recipe for disaster as you may eventually succumb to the temptation to write yourself a bigger part of the deal, to the detriment of your investors and your reputation.

Key Takeaways

For a table comparing the three waterfall models described in this chapter, that illustrates how each model affects distributable cash for investors and the asset management team, please go to: **https://RaiseCapitalForRealEstate.com/BonusMaterials.**

Figure out your split by determining overall cash on cash returns for a property. Once you know the overall projected return, you can decide how much you have to give investors and how much you need to keep for yourself. Try a couple of different splits until you land on one that gives your investors a return in the mid to high teens, without starving the management team during ownership of the property.

Keep a list of all your assumptions, as you'll need to list them in your property package or investment summary. Please be sure to write disclaimers into the offering documents that all of your assumptions could be wrong, but if you use reasonable, conservative assumptions, you should end up close unless something outside of your control goes wrong (such as a pandemic, interest rate hikes, etc.). Just make your best estimates, use the right disclaimers, and forge ahead.

Chapter 9

Creating Your Marketing and Operations Plan

Once you reach the point where an investor or group of investors is considering investing in a future Senior Living project with you, it's time to get serious. You've gotten your foot in the door; now, you need to show them a Senior Living project with a solid plan of operations and real numbers that they can invest in.

During your first few meetings with potential investors, you'll be expected to provide certain plan-oriented aspects of your endeavor. Among the most important of these is your operations plan describing how your business will operate and a marketing plan describing how you will fill the beds in your Senior Living property.

Marketing is a core concept that can determine whether your business fails or thrives. Without appropriate marketing or planning, your business will not reach consumers of your services (i.e., seniors in need of Senior Living housing and/or their families). And when that happens, your business will inevitably capsize. That is why having a solid marketing plan to attract residents to your property is so important to your potential investors.

To create an effective plan, you'll need to start by answering some important fundamental questions:

- How will your marketing plan support your business goals (i.e., to fill beds with residents who can afford to live there)?
- What is the mission you're trying to accomplish, and why?
- Who are you trying to reach with your marketing activities?
- Who is your competition, and where does your Senior Living property rank?
- What makes your Senior Living property unique?

- What will you charge residents, and how did you determine what to charge?
- How will you reach your target market and inform them of your Senior Living property?
- How much money will you spend, and on what?
- What tasks do you need to complete to reach your marketing goals?
- What results have you achieved (if applicable), and where can you improve?

If you've never run a business or created a marketing plan before, however, you probably won't know where to start with this.

Here are a few tips on how to get started with generating your marketing plan:

Begin With Your Executive Summary

The executive summary is usually included at the beginning of your marketing plan. It is a brief overview of your company and will include a list of your plan's key points. This is usually done in paragraph format with various headings and subheadings, but it can also include bullet points or numbered lists if necessary.

State Your Company's Values, Vision, and Mission

Before you begin what will undoubtedly be several pages' worth of marketing what if's, it's a good idea to first summarize your company's values, vision, and mission for your potential investors. This will help frame your marketing plan in a clear perspective.

The following is a simplified example of a Values, Vision, and Mission statement:

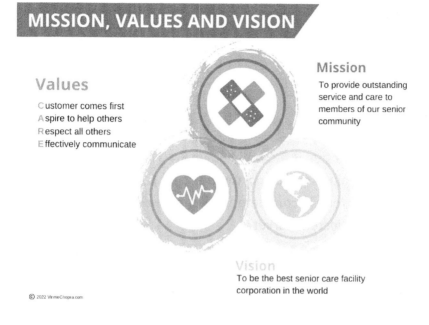

Naturally, you will want the phrases in your own statement to be much more unique and representative of your company goals. Use them as an opportunity to show your potential investors that you are passionate about the Senior Living industry and win them over.

Examine the Market and Competition

A good marketing plan is always backed up by solid evidence, and your potential investors know this. If you spout facts during your presentations that turn out to be false, it could ruin your chances both with those investors and in the Senior Living industry.

To start examining the external factors that could affect your marketing plan, spend some time analyzing your current market situation, looking at your competition, and applying what you learn to help mitigate your current strengths and weaknesses. Here are a few things you can research about your competitors to get started:

- Their leadership teams
- Their marketing tactics
- Their "selling points."
- Most loved amenities
- Their top-performing ads
- Their social media
- Their weak points

Also included in this step is the well-known SWOT analysis. SWOT stands for **Strengths, Weaknesses, Opportunities, and Threats.** As you conduct this analysis, you form a complete, unbiased view of the Senior Living business in your selected market.

Define Your Ideal Customer

Next on your marketing-outline to-do list will be identifying your ideal customer. In your case, this will be your ideal Senior Living resident and their families who will need to make Senior Living arrangements for their elder family members.

Anyone can say that their target audience is "families of senior citizens," but it's much more impressive to investors if you take the time to identify precisely who in that demographic you're talking to. Are you talking to the youngest daughter of a senior who is only 20 years old and is just getting out on her own? Likely not.

Rather, it's more likely you're targeting the eldest daughter or son who has had time on their own to experience the world. Instead of being in their early 20s, they're probably closer to their mid-to-late 30s or 40s and have established both families and careers of their own.

How do we know this? Well, let's look at some facts:

- First, if a person is looking for a quality Senior Living home for their parent(s) or grandparent(s), we can safely say that indicates a certain degree of maturity.

www.VinneyChopra.com/FreeBenefits

- Second, a young child in their early twenties will be busy enough trying to get on their own two feet. If they have an older sibling, the parents' living situation will likely be left in their hands.
- Third, we know that the family members seeking care for their parents have established families and careers because, if they hadn't, they would probably take on the task of caring for the elder family members themselves.

So, with that said, what do we do with this information? For you, the answer is to turn it into a full profile.

The most effective way to keep your marketing on track with the demands of your ideal customers is to ensure you know exactly who your ideal customer is. One way to do this is to imagine yourself in your target customer's head and create a mock resume that details important aspects of their lives.

As you work on this, I recommend using a **top-down strategy.** That is, start from least specific to most specific. This can be done in various ways, but the following is an excellent example of how it might appear in a marketing plan:

Identify Your Target Audience:

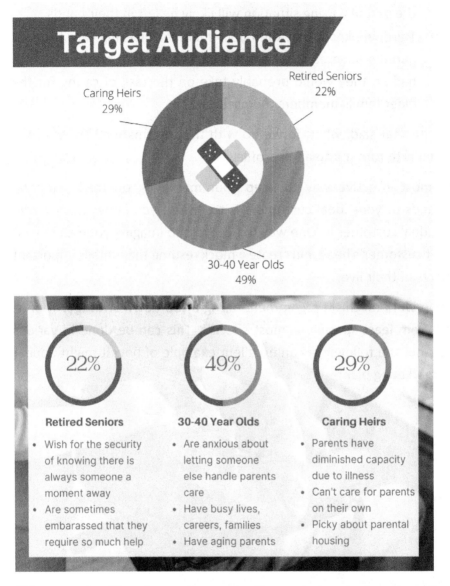

*Please note: The above does not allege what your target audience *should* be. It merely provides an example of what it *might* look like depending on your business plan, competition, geographical factors, and the type and level of care you plan to offer.

www.VinneyChopra.com/FreeBenefits

Once you've established your audience, it's time to narrow it down to one or multiple specific personas of the actual residents who might live in your Senior Living facility. I recommend having multiple of these, but I will provide an example of what one might look like:

Customer Persona

Gender: Male and Female | Age: 55-80 | Income: $55,000+

Habits:

-Likes to attend social events such as Bingo and Trivia nights

-Prioritizes personal healthcare

-Likes the peace and quiet of rural areas

Goals:

-Wants to stay socially connected with others in the same age group

-Wants help with basic tasks while maintaining some autonomy

-Wants to feel that they are still productive, even in retirement

Identify Your Marketing and Operations Goals

As you continue through planning, it is imperative that you not only identify clear, concise goals for yourself and your Senior Living business but also that you write them down. This will both help you as you forge your path through the Senior Living industry, as well as define your goals to your investors so that you can better persuade them that you and your planned Senior Living facility are a worthy investment.

For this portion of your plans, there are a few things you should keep in mind.

First, make sure that the goals you write down are quantitative instead of qualitative. In essence, make sure you're using tangible numbers instead of vague statements; and that the results are measurable.

For example, let's say that your goal is to give the elderly a higher quality living experience. Instead of stating that you'd like to give them a better living experience, you would jot down that you'd like to achieve a consistent satisfaction rating higher than 90%. This can be measured with periodic resident surveys, which can help you identify gaps or problems in operations, amenities, or staffing. Additional goals would include sharing your year-by-year income and expense projections and your sources and uses of funds describing where the money is coming from to develop or acquire and improve the project and how the money will be spent.

Be sure to create conservative operations goals for your Senior Living project. It's better to be conservative and over-deliver than it is to be overly optimistic and miss the mark. Remember to use the acronym "SMART." SMART stands for specific, measurable, attainable, relevant, and time-bound. As you're defining your goals, make sure each one applies to the above acronym for the best results. In most cases, framing your goals so that they can be expressed as a measurable percentage will satisfy these requirements. Then, to make it time-bound, simply add a deadline.

Here is a list of marketing goals you might consider adding to your marketing plan:

- Satisfaction ratings
- Occupancy goals
- Marketing campaign goals
- Staffing goals
- Expense and revenue goals

Operations Goals. Whether you are building your Senior Living facility from scratch (i.e., developing it), purchasing an existing building and converting it to a Senior Living facility, or simply buying an existing Senior Living facility outright, you must do a thorough property analysis. This analysis includes estimating the current and projected market value, planning and getting bids for specific renovations.

Carry out the proper due diligence on your potential property, including:

- Shopping the market for other Senior Living homes to determine possible rent rates, compare amenities, etc.
- Availability of mortgage financing; passive investors always want higher returns than bank financing, so all bank financing options should be fully explored.
- Doing the math and providing financial projections for both the period of ownership (to determine cash flow returns that can be shared with investors) and any proposed resale strategies (to determine equity that may be realized on resale and shared with investors).
- Inspecting the property and conducting feasibility studies to determine the best type of Senior Living facility to provide in that market.

- Checking the availability and rates for insurance so it can be factored into your financial projections.
- Conducting a staff salary survey in your area to determine what you will have to pay for the various levels of staff you will need to hire.

Present Your Operations Strategies to Investors

Now that you have your background details fledged out, it's time to present your plans to investors.

The most important thing at this point is to make sure you can answer any question an investor might throw at you regarding your plan of operations for the Senior Living facility they are investing in.

We recommend breaking down your operations strategies into phases. For a Senior Living facility, the phases of operation are:

- facility preparation,
- pre-opening,
- soft opening,
- hard opening, and
- post-opening.

Each one of these phases will require specific marketing strategies to generate and keep the public's interest.

The facility-preparation phase, for example, will involve things like floor planning, determining the number of beds, defining the amenities you'll provide, generating SOPs, deciding what operations staff you need, etc.

During the pre-opening phase, you might rent a "Coming Soon" billboard in your area, generate and send out a press release to local news organizations, double-check your SOPs and make sure there are no errors, and hire your staff. You'll also begin planning for your soft opening.

The soft-opening phase will follow. Soft openings for Senior Living homes function similarly to an open house. You'll have run marketing during the pre-opening phase, which will have already generated public interest and informed them of the open house.

During the soft opening, you'll allow members of the public and prospective residents to explore the facility, and you may even consider a short presentation on daily life, planned events, and amenities. By the end of this phase, your website should be available online for information and marketing purposes, and your social media accounts should be registered and active. Additionally, we recommend utilizing your open house to begin your email list. Simply have people sign it at the door with their names and email addresses to be added to the list. Once your soft opening has taken place, it's time for your hard opening.

A hard opening represents the date after which your facility is able to register, house, and care for residents. Marketing during this phase should be aimed at acquiring residents and promoting your facility and team as a leader in Senior Living and care.

Finally, you move into the post-opening phase. This phase occurs when you have a healthy number of residents actively housed and you want to maintain relevancy in the industry. You can also use marketing during this phase to build a waiting list for potential residents.

Define Your Marketing and Operations Budget

The last step of building your marketing and operations plans will involve detailing your budget. This will help you know how much to allocate to each marketing or operations strategy and will tell investors precisely where the income generated by the facility is going.

This is important so you don't lose sight of the financial implications of your project while getting caught up in the details of setting up and operating the facility. This will also help you decide how much to offer staff as payment and help you choose between paid service providers.

In the Senior Living space, you have the option of:

a. Running your Senior Living facility yourself and hiring support staff, or

b. Hiring a professional senior care operations manager to run your facility and provide support staff, or

c. Leasing your facility to a professional senior care management company, which may pay you a fixed rent or profit share.

Options b and c above can eliminate the stress, responsibility and, most importantly, help control the cost, but they will likely cost more as you will have to pay someone else to take on the role you would otherwise have if you self-managed the facility.

Consider who you're trying to reach with your marketing plan for the Senior Living project. Who is the specific audience? Elderly citizens? Their families? Investors? Once you've identified your target market(s), you will be better able to cultivate a plan that addresses their specific values, needs, and concerns. This is called your unique selling proposition (USP), which is what sets you apart from everyone else in the industry within your geographic area.

Here are the goals for each of the plans you will create:

- Your marketing plan should help you nail down the associated costs, such as website development, advertising, public relations, social media content, and internet marketing. If you're not comfortable taking on the task of marketing and promoting your facility (or don't have a dedicated in-house marketing team to do this for you), you can outsource to a third-party consultant or organization to help build, execute, and track your marketing plan for an additional cost. Be sure to assign a marketing budget to determine what marketing elements you can afford. Even a little marketing can go a long way in spreading the word about your facility and contributing to your profit margin.

- Your sources and uses of funds will help you determine startup and improvement costs for your facility. Once you know how much you need to spend to develop and/or acquire and improve the property, you can figure out how much will come from a bank loan. The remainder is the amount you need to raise from investors. This is the amount against which all of your ROI calculations will be made.

- Your operations plan will help you project annual income and expenses to help you determine whether the amount you are charging residents for rent is sufficient to pay the costs of property ownership (principal, interest, taxes, property insurance, etc.) and operations costs (staff salaries, utilities, liability insurance, materials, and supplies, etc.) plus generate a profit for your investors. In the operations plan, you should also describe the proposed exit strategy for you and/or your investors. Will you sell the property and business after a period of time? Will you refinance and buy out investors? What is your plan for giving investors their money back and giving them a share of the equity their funds created while they were invested in the project?

Chapter 10

Critical Elements of Managing a Senior Living Facility

Before you open your home to elderly residents, you need to know the licensing laws of the state your facility will be located in. Different states have different laws and regulations that guide Senior Living homes, with some being stricter than others. Certainly, there are lots of homes operating without licenses, but it's easier and far less costly to know the rules in advance of receiving state sanctions — or worse, getting shut down or fined for running an illegal facility; or losing your insurance and facing an uninsured loss. We will discuss staffing in a separate chapter.

Do All Assisted Living Facilities Need A License?

Yes, before opening, all assisted living communities must have a state-issued license. State agencies inspect these communities annually or when someone files a complaint. During these inspections, any violations or deficiencies are noted. Licenses can be suspended or even revoked for failure to comply with requirements.

A license shows that you are complying with the rules and regulations set by the state for the type of Senior Living facility you are offering, and it also helps you receive payment from insurance companies. Studies have shown that customers would rather patronize licensed and certified operators than unlicensed ones. Licenses are good for your business. Here are a few things that will be taken into consideration before a state grants you a license:

The Resident Rental Contract

Before admitting anyone into your Senior Living home, you should have a rental contract that protects you and your resident. A contract is legally binding, and it highlights what happens if either party defaults. It will explicitly state the rules and regulations of the facility, what is permitted and what is not permitted, fees and payment plan, and what happens in case of illness, death, or non-payment. The contract must highlight everything of importance in the Senior Living facility. Each party must agree, and documentation must be signed before any resident can move in. Always try to work within the confines of your contract to avoid any legal complications.

Rules and Regulations

The state in which your resident resides may check that you have created proper rules and regulations for your Senior Living facility and its occupants. The parameters of your rules must align with the type of Senior Living facility you've decided to establish; for example, the rules in a RAL home will be different from those in a full palliative care home. The number of residents will also help determine your rules and outline such things as visiting hours, number of visitors per visit, what you can bring into the facility, and feeding protocols, among other things.

Policies and Contingency Plans

Regardless of the state, state regulators will all want to know what policies and contingency plans you have created to keep your residents and the facility safe. What are your procedures in case of an emergency? What happens in case of a fire, storm, or power outage? Do you have adequate security? What are your SOPs? How is building and equipment maintenance handled?

Your Senior Living home must have written policies, and they may need to be approved. State agencies, while they do provide rules regarding certain procedures, do not provide the specific policies and procedures. You must facilitate the SOPs yourself. These SOPs contain details about how you plan to operate your Senior Living facility. Your SOPs are reviewed, and you will get a response as to whether they are acceptable.

Going forward, the state will hold you accountable for adhering to what you have stated in your SOPs.

Make sure you limit your SOPs to the ones that matter (important policies, emergency plans, and balanced meals). You may include other critical procedures with the help of your experienced manager.

Additionally, if you are hiring in-house staff, you will need a human resources program. Depending on the size of your Senior Living facility, you may need an off-site or in-house human resources manager.

Compliance

Knowing, understanding, and complying with state laws regarding your facility keeps you in good standing with your investors, community, insurance company, and, most importantly, your residents. There's no national website that lists the auditing and licensing history of Senior Living homes because they are regulated by the state, not by the federal government. Generally, each state has regulations, though the specifics of the requirements vary considerably from state to state. Typical regulations require:

- Resident agreements, informing potential residents on the associated costs of care (prior to move-in).
- Clearly defined resident admission and retention policies (based on needs and behavior).
- Support services and service plans which describe in detail the type of care provided to residents.
- Any required medication provisions and establishing who can administer or access them.
- Foodservice and dietary provisions, including dietary recommendations.
- Staffing requirements, including background checks, training, and continuing education.

- Apartment sizes, roommate rules, and number of people sharing a bathroom.
- Inspection, security, and monitoring requirements.
- Consequences for facilities that are non-compliant.

Business Expenses

Apart from startup capital, there are expenses attached to the smooth operation of your business. Your income will vary depending on the size of your home, resident rental rates, utilities, occupancy rate, and staff members. You will need a carefully controlled budget to run your business effectively.

Your budget for the day-to-day operations of your facility is, in many regards, like those items you would manage in a regular household, including food, phone, internet, cable, utilities, and maintenance. You will also need to factor in expenses such as license renewals, taxes, rent, and legal fees, and the cost of organized activities.

Staff wages are deductible business expenses for tax purposes. Depending on the size of your Senior Living facility, you will need a part- or a full-time bookkeeper as well as an independent CPA who will file your annual tax returns.

Choosing the Insurance Your Facility Will Accept

As you likely know, not all senior care facilities accept all insurance. Two of the most widely debated are Medicare and Medicaid.

Medicare

Medicare is the federal government program that provides health care coverage (health insurance), regardless of income, if you are:

- 65+
- Under 65 and receiving Social Security Disability Insurance (SSDI)

for a certain amount of time
- Under 65 with End-Stage Renal Disease (ESRD)

Both Medicare and Medicaid work together to offset costs and provide health coverage to those who need it most. However, Medicare does not pay for the following types of senior care:

- Assisted living.
- Long-term care at a nursing home.
- Residential care homes.
- Any long-term care.

Medicaid

Medicaid provides health coverage to millions of low-income Americans and is administered by states according to federal requirements. The program is funded jointly by states and the federal government.

Whereas Medicaid acts as a safety net for Americans who need care that they cannot afford privately. Like Medicare, Medicaid acts as health insurance, but it covers almost every type of healthcare cost and can also be used to pay for long-term nursing home care. As the owner of your Senior Living facility, you have the option of accepting Medicaid residents or not.

What to Consider Before Accepting Medicaid at Your Facility

Some of the potential residents who are Medicaid members might not have yet been approved for Medicaid when they come to your care home. If the application is denied, the initial costs for the first 90 days of their stay with you will not be covered, and you will have to cover the loss.

The reimbursement process can be lengthy, and even then, you might not be reimbursed in full; Medicaid can ask for a refund, even years after the resident has left your facility. You will require patience and slightly deeper pockets while you wait out the system.

Keep in mind, though, even though the Medicaid process can have cons, allowing Medicaid-paid residents into your facility provides more value to your community and makes your Senior Living facility more affordable and thus available to a wider group of potential residents.

Chapter 11

Hiring Staff

In this section, we'll drill down on one of the most essential components of your business, your staff, whom we will collectively call "caregivers." The success of your Senior Living business is dependent on more than your passion and good business acumen.

The employees at your Senior Living facility are the frontline of your business and interact with your residents every day. How skilled, agile, positive, and dedicated they are can either make or break your business; it's vital to surround yourself with staff that you can trust to carry out the tasks that need to get done with the level of excellence and the positive attitude that you require. Their attitudes will be a reflection of your own or that of your management team.

Below, we'll identify the key steps to finding, interviewing, hiring, developing, and evaluating qualified employees for your business. Depending on the type or size of Senior Living facility you have, there are certain categories of staff you should have on your payroll.

What Staff Do You Need?

In this industry, one of the most common ways to classify a Senior Living facility is by the levels of assistance provided. An active 75-year-old will not need the same kind of support and daily assistance as a less active 90-year-old with numerous health conditions; not all seniors have equal care needs.

It is extremely beneficial to know the market and exactly what part of that market you are striving to cater to. There are five basic levels of care and services provided to seniors, all of which offer specific levels of assistance: senior (55+) apartments, independent living, RAL, memory care, and skilled nursing.

The chart above illustrates the activities of daily living, or ADLs. These are the main areas that differentiate independent living from assisted living with regard to bathing, dressing, eating, mobility, and toileting.

Whether you are an owner, investor, or caregiver in the Senior Living industry, understanding the needs of the residents in each type of business model is important for determining your vision and, ultimately, the type of facility you will create. Knowing and anticipating the needs of potential residents in your community will go a long way to determining the success of your Senior Living facility.

Once you've decided which type of senior care facility you want based on the level of care you want your facility to provide, you can then make informed decisions about what types of staff will help you achieve those goals. Your Senior Living facility must be well-staffed for it to function properly. On-or Off-site managers, doctors, nurses, and certain in-house caregivers may be necessary to help residents who need assistance with bathing, getting dressed, feeding, movement, medical attention, and administering prescribed medication. You may also need dedicated kitchen staff, a maintenance crew, and janitorial services.

Your staff members are vital employees and offer services that extend far beyond executing day-to-day tasks. They interact with and engage your residents, and it's essential that you retain top-tier employees to ensure that your operations run smoothly. Your staff may do any of the following in the day-to-day operations of your facility:

- **Personal Care:** Bathing, dressing, eating, helping residents use the toilet, lifting residents out of bed.
- **Homemaking:** Preparing meals, cleaning, laundry, buying groceries and toiletries.
- **Medical Care:** Managing medication, physical therapy, intravenous treatments, dialysis, and physician's appointments (where applicable).

www.VinneyChopra.com/FreeBenefits

- **Emotional Care:** Companionship, conversation, social and enriching activities.

Below are job descriptions for various positions needed to run a Senior Living facility:

A Qualified Manager

To get your business started, you will need a qualified manager, preferably one that has a medical background. Your manager hires and oversees staff and takes care of all administrative affairs.

Some states have specific requirements and skill sets that your manager must possess before they will give your facility a license; some states will even require the completion of a course specially designed for managers of care homes. While you might be tempted to take on the role of manager yourself, we strongly advise that you hire someone who is qualified and has the experience needed to manage your home properly – at least until you learn the business and decide whether running a Senior Living facility is what you really want to do.

Personal Care Assistants (PCAs)

PCAs are not usually certified and have varying levels of experience, depending on the years they've spent in the industry. PCAs have conversations with the residents, provide companionship and walk with them. PCAs can also get involved in chores and activities, such as bathing or using the toilet, offering transportation to appointments, shopping, and more.

Check your state's provisions for hiring a PCA; for example, some states require that PCAs have extensive training, while the rules are more relaxed in other states. Note that for in-home care, PCAs are not generally covered under insurance and will require payment of a regular wage.

Home Health Aides (HHAs)

Unlike a PCA, HHAs must be trained and certified before they can work in your Senior Living facility. In addition to the tasks listed above, an HHA is trained to monitor the resident's vitals and observe medical conditions.

Licensed Nursing Assistants (LNAs Or CNAs)

The certification level required of a Licensed (or Certified) Nursing Assistant is much higher than that of a PCA or HHA, which directly reflects the importance of their job. CNAs help with personal care duties, including bathing, using the toilet, dressing, and mobility. They are tasked with monitoring the residents' vital signs, watching for health changes, and reporting any concerns that could compromise a resident's safety and welfare. CNAs are also trained to set up medical equipment, change dressings, take care of infections, and are able to offer more intensive, personalized health-based care to the residents.

Skilled Nursing Providers (SNPs)

SNPs must meet the federal standard for health and safety. They are licensed by the state and require years of training and education. They can offer care services and direct medical care that cannot be provided by any of the professionals listed above. For example, SNPs can administer drugs and shots, change wound dressings, care for residents with diabetes, and other medical-related tasks.

The Culinary Team

You have a wealth of options when it comes to finding people to round out your culinary team. However, hiring a top-tier food preparation team involves much more than finding chefs. There are a few things to keep in mind when making your selection; a successful Senior Living culinary team has unique and highly specialized qualities:

- **Service First:** Friendly and attentive service is just as important as nutritious and delicious food. The members of your Senior Living culinary team should be personable, polite, and attentive.
- **Versatility:** Seniors often eat personalized meals based on medical conditions, dietary requirements, or prescription medications. From low-sodium heart-healthy options to diabetic-friendly desserts, your team must be flexible, creative, and resourceful enough to prepare a range of fresh menu options.
- **Responsive to Feedback:** Residents must feel that they have a say in their dining experience. Culinary teams should create opportunities for input and feedback; even criticism is an opportunity to make senior residents feel validated and heard.

When you assemble the right culinary team, it can be rewarding and fulfilling for both the team and the Senior Living community they serve.

Salespeople

When done right, having well-trained salespeople can be the lifeblood of your business. These will be the people that really drive home the benefits of your facility.

To do this, consider hiring professional salespeople. Work with sales trainers to develop a standardized, mandatory training program for your salespeople. Use this program to highlight your facility's many benefits as well as provide sales tips, sales etiquette, and best practices. In a field like this, one false move from a salesperson (such as not demonstrating enough empathy) can create a poor image for your business and result in a loss of residents.

Additionally, consider having new salespeople shadow seasoned professionals so they can ask questions and learn the ropes more effectively. Make sure to periodically secret shop your salespeople. You can usually enlist a friend or colleague to do this for you. You want to know what they are saying when they don't think you are listening.

Home Care Employment Agencies

Home care employment agencies can give you referrals for various staff, such as nurses and health aides. One of the benefits of working with a home care employment agency is that they've conducted background screening on each person in their database. Additionally, these agencies can also provide worker training and occasional on-site supervision. The best home care agencies are run by people with relevant professional training and a genuine commitment to your resident's well-being.

Finding The Right Staff To Fit Your Specific Needs

If you are an owner or operator of a Senior Living home or facility, knowing the training and experience level that goes into each of the preceding roles gives you options for how to proceed with staffing your facility. Knowing what each role entails allows you to make informed decisions about the staff you interview and hire. Furthermore, you may decide that some hires in these roles are best suited as regular employees on your payroll, whereas others can be hired as independent contractors and take on a part-time or as-needed role. Regardless of what you choose, having a wide variety of competent, compassionate, well-trained professionals boosts your marketability and reputation for having and running a top-notch Senior Living facility.

It is also worth budgeting for more staff than you need at any one time. Having the bare minimum number of care staff needed to run your operation might become problematic if one of them becomes sick or unable to work; having additional options ensures that your residents don't experience any lapse in care.

Recruiting And Retaining Staff

Skilled, loving, certified, and dependable caregivers are the key to a well-run operation. Caregivers are the heart and soul of any quality Senior Living facility — they reflect your brand and are critical to your reputation in this industry. You want to be known as the place that employs the best caregivers who provide superior care to your residents. Your staff must treat residents with care, dignity, and respect, and they must be empowered to problem solve as well as take direction — a tall order for any employee.

In addition to finding quality managers and caregivers, it is also important to find reliable, professional independent contractors to execute specific tasks or who can be called on an as-needed basis. You'll want contractors who interact with residents or staff with respect and a positive attitude. Having a reliable maintenance contractor (or several) to address issues with the property is essential.

Keeping your Senior Living facility clean and in good shape is vital for ensuring the health of your residents and critical for preventing the spread of infection. In many Senior Living residences, caregivers will share housekeeping duties, although you may want to hire separate cleaning staff (budget permitting) so that your caregivers can focus their time and expertise on the physical and mental needs of your residents.

Recruiting: What To Look For

While a caregiver's role will change based on their job title, licensing, and role in your Senior Living facility, the basic, inherent qualities you should look for will remain the same:

- **Positive attitude:** Quality caregivers should always have a positive attitude, even in a challenging or frustrating situation. A positive attitude will also affect the spirit and well-being of your seniors, making them feel active and happy.

- **Passion for relationship-building:** Although caregivers take care of the physical needs of senior citizens, a quality caregiver also works to create an interpersonal relationship with their elderly charges and attends to both their emotional and mental needs.
- **Taking initiative:** A quality caregiver is the eyes and ears of your elderly residents and their families; they view their role as helping the family members watch over and care for their loved ones from a distance. A good caregiver will address any concerns before they become problems and actively work to solve them.
- **Patience:** Caring for seniors requires a lot of patience; they often work at a different pace and, in some cases, a different level of understanding. A good caregiver has patience in abundance and is never short or quick to lose his temper with an elderly resident.
- **Helping seniors gain a sense of independence:** Seeing a senior's strengths, abilities, and potential is the difference between a good caregiver and a great one. By engaging your resident's strengths, you not only give them back their dignity, but you reestablish that these are people, not just "residents."

Staff Compensation and Retention

Your staff and caregivers are vital employees and offer services that extend far beyond executing day-to-day tasks. They interact with and engage your residents, and it's essential that you retain top-tier employees to ensure that your operations run smoothly.

You will generally conduct a market survey to determine how much you will pay per hour. To determine your pay rate, research the wages offered by local home care agencies. Employment benefits can also make the job more attractive to potential applicants, as well as help with staff retention. Some benefits you might offer include:

- Paid vacation days.
- Paid sick days.

www.VinneyChopra.com/FreeBenefits

- Dental Insurance.
- Health insurance.
- Tuition for healthcare education.

Put your staff in your shoes. The business becomes theirs just as it is yours. They will represent the owner in different aspects of the business. You want them to be like clones of your ideal staff member, making all the right key decisions, even when you or your manager aren't there.

How to Attract a Diverse Workforce

In today's workforce, you need to ensure a diverse workforce to succeed. Diversity is important, and your hiring managers (and you) need to be aware of it, but finding the right staff to meet the needs of your residents should take precedent over trying to meet a quota. The best way to be inclusive is to make sure that your advertising is generic and inclusive and that you seek qualified candidates that meet the job description and have the right, positive attitude without regard to names, gender, age, race, religion, or any other bias that may exclude certain demographics from becoming valued team members. There are a few ways you can do this:

Look past degrees. Especially for entry-level roles, transferable skills from previous jobs will be much more important than classroom-only training. Prioritize candidates that have real-life experience in the field and hire those who have a combination of solid potential talent and hands-on experience. Offer to train people with the right attitudes.

Seek out talent from nontraditional sources. Most workplaces source their talent from online and digital advertisements. They may also partner with talent-sourcing websites like Indeed or Glassdoor. However, an excellent option for solid talent is partnering with nontraditional sources such as not-for-profit workplace development training providers.

Identify key skills. An excellent way to seek out candidates is to determine the top 5 skills the job in question requires and identify similar jobs that use the same skills. For example, you might consider candidates from home health care or Hospice providers.

Limit skills on job postings. When you list skills on job postings, prospective candidates who have similar skills or lack even just a few of those you've listed may not apply. Limit the number of skills you list to only those that are required so that you can avoid omitting important talent. Also, include language in your ad that says that you are willing to train if that's within your facility's capability.

Use gender-neutral language. To avoid inadvertently discouraging talent of one gender or another from applying, make sure you use gender-neutral language in all job postings.

Standardize your interview process. Include multiple steps to the interview process with a group of diverse individuals to get a well-rounded opinion on a potential candidate. Eliminate any hiring process that hinges on a single decision-maker to eliminate unnecessary bias.

Chapter 12

Choosing An Operator for Your Facility

Lessee/Operator

One alternative to hiring and managing your own staff is to lease the property to a Senior Living operator. Leasing the property out to an operator makes your investment more like a real estate investment than running a business. In this instance, the operator would pay a fixed monthly rent to the property owner, or each of the residents would pay rent to the property owner while paying a separate amount to the operator for their care.

Paid Management Company

Another alternative to hiring your own in-house staff is to hire an assisted living management company that will oversee the operation of the business, including staffing, marketing for residents, schedules, and other essential activities required to run the business efficiently (and profitably). In this case, the property owner would collect the rent from residents and would pay the management company a monthly fee as part of its operating expenses.

In both cases, the selected manager or operator should specialize in Senior Living properties, with at least five years of experience in the Senior Living industry.

Where Can You Find Operators or Managers?

You may find operators through Residential Assisted Living Conferences, where operators are seeking real estate investors and vice versa. As an owner seeking an operator, you should be very careful in making your selection. Your decision should be based on industry experience, a track record based on reviews from residents in other facilities they manage, references from other Senior Living facility owners, and financial strength.

The operator or management company you choose will influence several important factors regarding your business, such as:

- Whether you have sustainable success and profitability
- The efficacy of your marketing
- The follow-through of your staff
- The successful implementation of your business model
- The reputation of your Senior Living Facility

In the real estate business, reputations are everything. Your operator needs to be able to create and foster important relationships, so it's imperative that you properly vet and hire the right candidate(s).

How to Vet a Senior Living Operations Manager

Vetting a Senior Living operations manager requires gathering information about their background and experience, checking references, and researching their reputation in the Senior Living industry. As you vet your operators, be sure to ask the following questions to get a better understanding of who you could be working with:

Question #1: What Are Some Other Properties The Company Is Working With?

Your operator could be a part of a larger company or a standalone Senior Living management specialist. In either case, you want to understand what other properties they have managed.

Asking this question will tell you two things: First, you'll be able to gauge whether they have the capacity to take on new projects. If they already have too many projects, it may be in your best interest to seek out someone else.

www.VinneyChopra.com/FreeBenefits

Second, it will give you an understanding of where their expertise lies. It may be difficult for you to find an operator with experience in the Senior Living field, but someone who has managed multifamily investment properties could potentially apply that knowledge to the real estate side of your project. On the other hand, someone who primarily focuses on self-storage might not be the best choice. Ideally, you want someone with prior Senior Living experience or specialized training in Senior Living projects.

Question #2: Is The Operator Competent?

This question is more of one that you ask yourself as you find out more about your potential operations manager. It is crucial that your operator knows what they're doing in the Senior Living industry so that you can maximize the success of your project.

To get a better idea of how competent your potential operator is, look at the following factors:

- Do they have a track record of successful similar projects?
- Have they executed projects like this before?
- Have they ever nullified a management contract mid-project or exited early? If so, why?
- What do other property owners they've worked for have to say about them?

Asking these questions is the best way to ensure that your operator knows their way around a project like yours– and that they aren't just blowing smoke.

Question #3: What Is Their Management Philosophy?

To maximize your chances of success, you want your investment philosophy and your operator's investment philosophy to align. This means that you need to have the same expectations regarding staff treatment of residents, financial handling, reputation management, cleanliness, etc. Things run much more smoothly if everyone has the same goals, and your portfolio will thank you.

Question #4: What Do Their References Say?

If you ask for your potential operator's portfolio, the chances are high that they'll have several references listed. Don't shy away from contacting these references.

Tip: There are also real estate forums where investors can review and share information on Senior Living operators they've worked with. Try searching for your operator on these forums to get a better idea of how they work.

If you follow these steps, the chances of selecting the right operator for your Senior Living facility will be significantly increased.

Your Manager is the Eyes and Ears of Your Business

Whether it's you or a third-party manager, your operations manager is the person with the most responsibility. They will be overseeing the day-to-day operations, interacting with residents and their families, and representing your brand. In many cases, the manager can be responsible for finding, interviewing, hiring, evaluating, and firing staff. They can also be responsible for marketing your business, maintaining occupancy, and maintaining the reputation of your Senior Living facility.

A manager needs to be personable, empathetic, and gentle with your elderly residents. Managers need at least a basic understanding of human resources as they will be recruiting, training, and retaining caregiving staff. They will also need sharp business acumen to keep records, maintain stock of inventory and supplies, contract maintenance, and other services.

Managers will attract new residents, give tours, and develop relationships with prospective residents and their families. Additionally, they will troubleshoot problems with staff, the facility, or residents. Depending on how you decide to set up your facility, an effective manager can also be responsible for providing entertainment and stimulating your residents by organizing group activities such as yoga, exercise, arts and crafts, karaoke, movie nights, card games, etc. Ultimately, your manager is continually dealing with people; as such, the person you hire needs to be a real 'people person.'

Bonus: Work On Your Business, Not In It

I've seen people slave in their businesses, and I have seen people run their businesses successfully without involving themselves in the day-to-day operations of it. Personally, I think the latter is a better choice. It is always a good idea to make yourself available when you are needed. However, it is better to delegate tasks to your employees and give them the authority to make decisions without you present. That's why you hired them in the first place, and they are getting paid for it. Perhaps as a business owner, you want to have time for your family and enjoy the income from your Senior Living facility as an investment. This is the path you must determine. For example, I live a relatively free life compared to all-in business owners, and I can do other important things in my life. However, in order to do so, you must make sure you're putting the right people in charge of your business. This style of management doesn't take away your decision power as a business owner. You call the shots, but you have people to execute them in your stead.

Meanwhile, your managers must be empowered to make vital decisions in your absence. They interact with your residents and their families on a regular basis. How effective they are is key to giving you the freedom you desire in your journey to a successful REAL home business. Family members also must make key decisions with respect to seniors opting to live in your Senior Living facility. If your employees have an affable relationship with prospective and current residents, you'll be cementing the trust they have in your service.

Your job is to work on gaining perspective as a business owner so that you can make good decisions in your business, including whom to hire and what authority to give them. You should oversee and make key decisions, not micro-manage and make the day-to-day decisions. This is the model that will allow you to scale your Senior Living business so it can grow rapidly into developing additional Senior Living homes.

Chapter 13

Create a Referral Network

Marketing creates awareness for your business and your brand; it lets people know what you have to offer and why they should choose you over another provider. Depending on your marketing strategy, there are several resources you can employ to reach your target demographic:

- **Build a website:** One of the best ways to market your Senior Living home is with the aid of a website, an essential strategy for online marketing. There's no need to do this yourself; there are hundreds of website design firms that will gladly build a website for you.

- **Create social media accounts:** social media is a quick, cost-effective way of distributing information about your company and can create recognition for your brand. Platforms such as Facebook, LinkedIn, Twitter, and Instagram are frequently used to promote businesses and boost productivity while encouraging loyalty among your customers. These platforms are also ideal for referrals, posting testimonials, and advertising unique content.

- **Print and distribute flyers or brochures:** Printed materials are a quick and efficient way to distribute information about your facility. Survey your target neighborhood to see if there are any businesses that will let you leave flyers or brochures at or near their front desk or consider having a mailing service distribute flyers according to specific zip codes.

- **Business Cards:** Business cards are still one of the most important ways to advertise your Senior Living home. Literally a "calling card" for you and your business, a business card is a portable and efficient way to relay your services to a prospective resident or their families.

- **Signage:** This can include posters, billboards, and signage in front of your Senior Living facility. Creative, attractive, and eye-catching brand names and signs are a quick and efficient way to visually sell your brand.
- **Open Houses:** Having periodic well-organized and well-promoted open houses as a marketing strategy is not only cost-effective but also an efficient way of meeting potential residents and their families. It allows them to learn more about the services you have to offer.
- **Referrals:** Referral marketing is a strategy that adopts the use of recommendations to increase your resident base through word of mouth, ideally from existing residents or their families. It is a convenient (and free) means of informing people about the services and accommodations you offer. A satisfied resident will refer other residents, which can increase your occupancy rate. Referral marketing is a way to get your biggest supporters to help broadcast the name of your company and turn your existing residents into advocates.
- **Relationships:** Relationship marketing builds long-term relationships with potential and existing residents and other referral sources. The objective is to foster a reliable emotional connection to aid in marketing your Senior Living home.

In some situations, the role of building a relationship with residents, their families, and potential referral sources should be handled by your manager. If you are appointing a manager to oversee the job of fostering and encouraging customer loyalty, he or she must be able to connect effectively with the community.

Some key points to remember when building positive relationships with residents and their families include:

- Open and honest communication.

- Be friendly, social, and open to feedback.
- Communication through social media platforms, email, and in-person interactions.
- Provide personalized resident support and top-notch service.

Marketing to Hospices

Hospice focuses on quality of life and helping a person live as fully as possible despite a terminal illness. Many Senior Living communities are providing increasing levels of hospice care. In many states, terminally ill residents can receive hospice care, or end-of-life care, without leaving their Senior Living community.

Senior Living communities and hospice caregivers can work collaboratively to give residents the best end-of-life care possible. Hospice providers offer physical and emotional comfort to residents during their final months, weeks, or days. They also support family members as they navigate difficult decisions and the grieving process. By providing these services in Senior Living, residents can spend their last days in the comfort of their own homes. Currently, there are four states that don't allow hospice care to be provided in a Senior Living community, whereas hospice care is allowed at the discretion of the senior community in other states.

Once a resident needs hospice, the Senior Living community and the interdisciplinary team can work to create an organized care plan. Hospice care at Senior Living homes is covered by Medicare and most private health insurance plans. The Medicare hospice benefit covers the care team, equipment, medications, and therapies. Medicaid can provide coverage as well.

There are many benefits to working in tandem with hospice care, which is why it is vital to foster a relationship with hospice companies. Referral marketing is a great way to connect with these agencies; it provides a gateway through which you can deliver your value proposition and highlight the services you offer. Consider targeted, content-specific blogs and email newsletters that describe the value of hospice work and how it could enrich the quality of life at your Senior Living facility.

Addressing and Marketing to a Homeowner Association

A Homeowner Association (HOA) is an organization in a subdivision, planned community, or condominium that creates and enforces rules for property and residents who live there. Those who purchase property within an HOA's jurisdiction become members automatically and are required to pay dues (HOA fees).

It's not unusual for Senior Living residences to pop up in HOAs. What differs from association to association is the way they're maintained and how seamlessly they fit into the existing community. Some associations can be very restrictive about what members can do with their properties.

The trend towards group homes in residential neighborhoods is growing across the country; in particular, assisted living facilities for seniors, which are popular because they're small and allow personal care in a family-like setting. Still, HOAs will be quick to point out concerns over traffic, parking, and (senior) safety concerns. Fortunately, State Fair Housing Protection (the Fair Housing Act) covers all 50 states, including the District of Columbia. The FHA protects tenants from discrimination, which means that HOAs have no agency or authority over assisted living facilities. They do, however, require that they comply with required governing documents, including insurance or licenses that will protect the association and the neighborhood.

When dealing with the HOA, it's best practice to maintain a courteous, respectful relationship and provide 100% transparency into the facets of your operation. Listen to their concerns and offer insight into how you plan to address them. Invite your neighbors to attend an open house and offer discounts for HOA residents and their family members. Provide a dedicated space for HOA rules and regulations on your website (though remember that paying or compensating board members is strictly forbidden). When HOA members feel heard and seen, they will be more amenable.

Senior Placement Agencies

Deciding where to place a loved one can be a daunting task. Finding a facility that addresses the senior's health, budget, and location concerns can feel overwhelming to seniors and their families, which is why there are professional senior placement agencies that have the expertise and resources to help find suitable Senior Living facilities. These agencies provide placement services tailored to meet the needs of seniors, working directly with them or with their families to evaluate their specific situation and determine the best fit.

Though some placement services may request placement fees, there are many agencies that provide these services free of charge. Generally, they receive compensation from the communities or facilities to whom they refer residents, which is why marketing to senior placement agencies should be a key part of your marketing plan. Consider allowing placement agents to tour your facility, even during pre-construction; listen to their comments and suggestions, which will ultimately benefit potential residents. You can also offer incentives like referral bonuses for any resident referred to your facility to increase occupancy and boost the image of your facility.

Word-of-Mouth Referrals from Current Residents

By far, the most effective marketing tool you'll use is word-of-mouth marketing. People trust the advice and recommendations from their friends and family, which is why referral-based recommendations will always garner more residents than any other traditional marketing method.

To help bolster these word-of-mouth referrals, it's an excellent idea to create some sort of automated patient referral system.

Here are some steps you can take to create a resident-generating referral system for your location:

Tenant Satisfaction Surveys

Send an automated email to residents and their family spokespeople a specified length of time after a resident moves in. Ask questions that help prompt specific thoughts about their experience so that you can better understand their sentiments and improve customer relations.

This will help you understand how your residents and their families feel about your Senior Living home; and what caused them to choose your facility over others. This information can provide you with actionable items for improvement. Over time, this will also assist with resident retention as you are able to continuously understand and improve upon your intake process.

Automate Tenant Referrals

Use the findings you gather from your surveys to automate the resident referral process. Essentially, once the survey is filled out, a resident or their family will receive one of two emails: if they are happy with their experience, they receive a referral email that prompts them to refer others. Let them know you are happy to hear they are having a good experience and include an automated option that helps the individual send the referral via email to their friends and family.

On the other hand, if a person is not satisfied with their experience, they should receive a follow-up email or call that offers to solve their issues one way or the other. Either they are afforded a discount or deal, or you offer to have a face-to-face meeting so that you can get a better understanding of the issue. People love to know their feedback is taken seriously.

Offer Incentives

Not everyone will be willing to give up their valuable time to fill out a survey; in fact, most won't. To increase the likelihood that a person fills out their survey, you can offer incentives.

For example, you can offer discounted meals, living expenses, or specific luxuries for a month in exchange for a referral. It's important to get creative with your incentives, though, be sure to check with your local and state laws to ensure the incentives you're offering are permissible.

Use Current Residents As Brand Ambassadors

Your current residents will always be your most trustworthy voice. Others considering moving into your community or placing a family member in your community will want to hear from your current residents so they can accurately gauge the current living situation.

We recommend approaching some of your more vocal residents about being brand ambassadors. If they accept, their job will be things like giving tours of their living spaces, hosting leads at meals, providing testimonials, speaking at open house-type events hosted on the premises, and more. In exchange, you'd provide them with steeply discounted living quarters and other compensation.

Of course, the way you employ this tactic will vary depending on what level of care your facility offers. If you have a higher level of care, then it may be necessary to approach the family of your resident to do this job instead of the resident themself.

Manage Your Online Reputation

Too many businesses make the mistake of not paying enough attention to their reviews. However, an essential part of marketing is ensuring the community has good things to say about your business.

Think about it: If you had recently moved to a new area and you were looking for somewhere to have dinner, would you rather dine at a restaurant with two stars on Google or one with five stars and raving reviews? The answer seems simple, doesn't it?

Your residents are going to have the same mindset, perhaps an even more critical one than you. After all, this is their loved one's life– they're going to want to make sure everything is perfect.

To manage your online reputation, keep an eye on the reviews and comments left on your Google business page and your social media. If you see bad reviews, take them under consideration and figure out if there's a way you can improve from it. Additionally, consider reaching out to the person who posted the review to offer to meet with them. Then, apologize and let them know what changes you're implementing based on their feedback. You may even consider offering them some sort of discount or compensation for their heartache.

Always make sure to reply publicly to reviews. For good reviews, thank the person for taking the time to leave a review and how much you appreciate it. For bad reviews, be gracious and apologetic. Make sure you let them know you will be reaching out to them to help resolve the problem – and then *do it!*

Host Events for Residents and Prospects

For Senior Living communities, special events can make all the difference. Not only will it give your current residents something to look forward to, but potential residents can also attend and check out the facility without any expectations of being "sold to."

www.VinneyChopra.com/FreeBenefits

Additionally, your current residents will have the chance to chat with potential residents and talk about their experiences at your facility. As we've said before, this type of word-of-mouth marketing makes all the difference.

Chapter 14

Planning and Implementing Senior Activities

We've already covered how marketing is the lifeblood of Senior Living syndications and how word-of-mouth is the lifeblood of marketing. We've also discussed how to go about promoting word-of-mouth marketing– that is, all the little tips, tricks, and tactics you can use to promote the discussion of your business.

Ultimately, though, word-of-mouth isn't a proverbial pot that you should always have your hand in. Rather, it should work for you in the background while you spend your time on more management-intensive activities.

The best way to ensure frequent word-of-mouth referrals is, of course, to provide excellent service. Provide your elders with everything they need to be happy, fulfilled, and content, and their families *will* hear about it.

However, if you are providing excellent service to your seniors simply for marketing benefits, you probably shouldn't be in this business. Regardless of how it benefits your business, you should be providing the best quality of life to your seniors because they are the generation that provided for you, and they deserve the utmost luxury in these later years.

Now, with all that said, let's talk about one of the best ways to put seniors in a consistently positive mindset: it is to fill your monthly calendar with tons of stimulating activities. These, of course, will be optional for the seniors to attend but also highly encouraged.

Over time, having these activities in place and emphasizing them to new and potential residents can double or even triple your inhabitant rates. And just to remind you of what you stand to gain by raising your inhabitant rates:

79% occupancy means having 79 rooms filled out of the 100 on your premises. This leaves 21 rooms empty per month. At $800 per month per living space, those 21 empty living spaces cost you *$16,800 per month or over $200,000 per year.*

Now, with that said, let's look at how to earn that extra 200K.

Starting Your Activities Program

Don't get us wrong– starting an activities program for someone who is relatively new to the Senior Living scene isn't going to be a cakewalk. In fact, it will probably be quite a challenge at first as you work to navigate scheduling issues, event staffing, and resourcing. Fortunately, creating a quality program will get easier each time you do it until it is eventually no challenge at all.

Ultimately, the key to creating an effective activities program is to remember that every activity should have some sort of benefit. Each one should have meant stemming from both the nature of the activity itself and the way your staff handles said activity.

Additionally, an effective activities program should aim to improve the quality of life of your resident seniors. And while the term "quality of life" can sometimes be subjective, we use it to refer to improving a senior's mental and physical well-being while also enhancing their dignity and self-esteem.

In many cases, a lack of activities in a Senior Living community can contribute to a feeling of hopelessness and helplessness. Residents themselves commonly express how a lack of activities can stimulate a lack of purpose. Having activities in place gives them the freedom to have some choice in their schedules and helps them feel as though they are contributing to their community.

And this isn't just our opinion, either. Studies have shown that having recreational activities in Senior Living centers helps to:

- Reduce mental illnesses such as depression and anxiety, as well as cabin fever.
- Stimulate a sense of dignity and independence!
- Combat loneliness
- Provide structure, normalcy, and a sense of control.

Essentially, what we're saying is this: no matter what your budget constraints are, how new you are to the industry, or how lost you feel, forgoing the implementation of activities for your residents should never be an option. They are simply too important to your residents' quality of life.

So, since this next section is a requirement, let's move right into it:

What to Consider when Creating a Senior Activities Program

One of the things that makes creating a senior activities program so difficult is the factors you must consider for each activity. When social directors for Senior Living establishments consider the activities they want to implement, they must consider one thing above all else: the physical and cognitive limitations of the residents.

To best understand where your residents' limitations lie, we recommend spending some time with your nursing staff. They will be able to provide valuable insight in this regard.

And even if you aren't personally making the program yourself, we still recommend doing this. It's important to understand these limitations even if you are just the final step in your program's approval process.

Additionally, be sure to consider your residents':

- Personalities
- Preferences
- Capabilities

- Demeanor
- And more

Furthermore, consider what value your activities will hold. What will your residents take away? *How will they benefit?*

Four Activity Types for Seniors

To further simplify the process of creating your activity program, we're going to break down the activity types into four simple categories: **physical, social, creative, and mental.**

As you create your activities calendar for the months ahead, we recommend keeping the balance of each type by allotting 25% of the activity split to each type. That is, a quarter of your calendar will be social activities, a quarter of physical activity, and so on.

Seeing these numbers, it may also be tempting to use the four weeks in a month to your advantage and give each type a full week, but we do not recommend doing this. Having a week's worth of any single activity type in a row can be disastrous and lead to burnout or even a feeling of ostracization for those seniors who can't participate in those activity types. (For example, an immobile senior during a week of physical-only activities).

Unfortunately, other than this, we don't have any solid guidelines for how to arrange your activity spread. After all, the spread that will work best for your establishment will likely not work for another establishment of a different size.

Not only that, but your activity schedule is also highly dependent on the level of care you implement. If your seniors need to be supervised 100% of the time, you'll have less time for activities as you work to keep them on schedule. On the contrary, of course, seniors who are largely independent might like having several activities a day (perhaps even one of each type) to choose from.

Ultimately, you must look at your overall business plan and resident preferences and make those judgments for yourself.

1. Physical Activities

The need for physical activity only increases as we age to keep both our bodies and minds sharp.

In fact, a study conducted in 2003 by the University of Illinois confirmed, without a doubt, that exercise improves cognitive abilities, perhaps even more so than physical ones. The question is, to what extent?

This study found that four major variables had the most relation to the amount of improvement seniors saw:

- **Age:** Past the point of middle adulthood, the level of cognitive benefit we get from exercise increases exponentially.
- **Gender:** Females tend to benefit more from later-age exercise than males.
- **Exercise Type:** The best type of exercise for improving cognition at later ages appears to be aerobic exercise combined with mild resistance training.
- **Time Spent:** Time spent exercising also has a large effect on the level of benefit you derive. Those who exercise longer receive a greater benefit.

That said, there will be some forms of exercise that are better for your elders than others due to physical limitations. Your job is to balance the risk with the reward and create exercise programs that provide the most benefit to your seniors.

Additionally, one of the most beneficial exercise programs for seniors (and one we highly recommend) is a combination of aerobic and resistance training.

Over the past decade, several studies have been conducted to determine the true effect of this combination of targeted exercise in seniors. *Nearly all of them have found that it is the most effective recipe for cognitive improvement.*

One of the most important studies in this regard, though, is one conducted in 2012 with 70- to 80-year-olds with Mild Cognitive Impairment. This study found that twice-per-week resistance training could lead to significant benefits to attention and memory.

For those unaware, Mild Cognitive Impairment is only a short stage away from progressing to Dementia. Without any sort of intervention, 20% of those diagnosed with this illness will progress to full-blown Dementia within a year. The remaining 80% will do the same within six years.

When aerobic and resistance training are thrown into the mix, though, these statistics change drastically. With only twice-a-week training, this decline can be halted or even partially improved!

To help get your brainstorming started on what sorts of physical activities you can implement, here is a short list we've compiled that has shown to be particularly effective:

- Chair yoga/regular yoga
- Tai Chi
- Qi Gong
- Gardening
- Zumba or spin classes
- Water aerobics
- Dance
- Nintendo Wii Fit
- Croquet
- Walking/Gentle hiking
- Botanical garden tours

2. Social Activities

Building meaningful relationships while living in Senior Living facilities can be a daunting and sometimes difficult task for residents. Social activities can be an excellent way to foster relationships between your residents and make them feel more a part of the community.

And that's not the only benefit your residents stand to source from social activities. **Research** has also found that partaking in social events can also:

- Improve the quality of sleep and ability to fall asleep.
- Maintain motivation and physical function.
- Help reduce cognitive decline.

Some of the most common senior social activities for Senior Living facilities are:

- Birthday parties
- Holiday celebrations
- Reading groups
- Group learning activities.
- Religious services
- Arts and crafts
- Game nights
- Ice cream socials

3. Creative Activities

Creative activities are an excellent combination of physical and mental that help stimulate fine motor skills and hand-eye coordination. Depending on the event, creative activities can also provide cognitive stimulation.

Additionally, these types of activities can be especially helpful in seniors with Dementia, Mild Cognitive Impairment (MCI), Alzheimer's, anxiety, depression, and sundowner's syndrome. Some creative activities to consider include:

- Painting
- Sewing
- Crochet
- Paper crafting
- Origami
- Decorating cakes and other baked goods
- Pottery
- Flower arranging
- Fruit carving
- Jewelry making
- Wind chimes
- Woodworking/woodturning
- Fashion shows

4. Mental Activities

Your establishment's mental activities will work to keep your seniors sharp and engaged. In addition, these types of activities can slow down the progression of various cognitive impairments and help your residents feel independent.

Moreover, having *group* mental activities can help your residents be more involved with each other. Over time, this fosters friendship and helps your residents build relationships to help them remain content.

Consider the following as a basis for mental activities:

- Community trivia nights
- Learning instruments
- Genealogy
- Card games such as bridge
- Board games

- TED talks
- Computer classes
- Writing workshops
- Museum visits

Community Partnerships

What community businesses or brands could your Senior Living facility partner with?

It can be a daunting process to reach out to a brand or business you have little to no connection with. Most businesses want to give back, and some may welcome the opportunity to give back to seniors in their own community. Luckily, the list of partnership-worthy activities and services is wide and varied, so you shouldn't have much trouble finding *someone* willing to partner with you.

In general, the partner-able activities to consider can be broken down into five categories:

- Education and spiritual learning
- Exercise
- Health management
- Food and nutrition
- Intergenerational programs

Let's use this list to explore the types of establishments you can partner with and the programs/amenities you can set up with them:

For General Education:

- Local schools/colleges
- Office supply stores (for writing materials, printers, projectors, etc.)
- Local libraries or bookstores (for reading material)
- Craft stores (for craft materials)

For Spiritual Education

Education for seniors—whether general or spiritual—is incredibly important. General learning keeps the mind active and strong, reducing the progression of diseases like Dementia and Alzheimer's. At the same time, spiritual learning keeps the mind soothed and prevents/reduces the symptoms of mental illness like anxiety and depression.

In later years, it's common for seniors to want to either get more in touch with their religion or explore new ones. Having different worship opportunities, transport to local churches, or even a religion counselor on staff can help.

- Local churches (for transportation/religious text donations)
- Religious stores (for various religious items like rosaries, crystals, candles, head coverings, etc.)
- Local transport companies

For Physical Exercise

It comes as no surprise that exercise is incredibly important to maintaining a senior's quality of life. In recent years especially, there has been a tremendous amount of research focused on understanding how exercise affects cognition as we age.

Luckily, there are many, *many* establishments willing to donate or partner to fund exercise programs for seniors. Depending on the type(s) of exercise program you decide to implement (we'll cover more on this in the next section), you'll want materials such as yoga mats, volunteer instructors, barbells, resistance bands, sweat bands, ankle weights, etc.

Fitness establishments you can partner with:

- Yoga studios
- Local gyms
- Fitness centers (especially senior fitness centers)

- Athletic stores
- Pools or local swim teams
- Gardening stores

It may also be worth it to consider talking to local martial arts studios depending on the activity level of the seniors you serve. Certain martial arts studios may be willing to partner with you even though your seniors may need a lower-impact version of the martial arts they offer in their studios.

Health-Related Partnerships

In terms of senior health management, there are many different facets to keep in mind. In addition to physical health, you also must manage the emotional and mental strain seniors undergo and actively work to mitigate the effects.

Because health management is such a broad topic, it's difficult to say exactly who you should look to partner with or what activities you should add to your roster.

Ideas for Senior Activities

Here are a few senior activities to consider:

- Monthly picnics
- Playhouse trips
- Art shows with resident art
- Karaoke
- Flea market trips
- Park visits

You can find a longer list of activities in the next section, titled *Planning and Implementing Senior Activities.* For now, each item on this list should hit on the major points of self-care in some way or another, whether that be mental, physical, or emotional. Simply pick an activity and brainstorm who you could partner with to make that program happen.

Food And Nutrition-Related Activities

Like exercise, food and nutrition are both instrumental in maintaining one's health– especially for seniors. In fact, many illnesses and ailments we experience in our adult lives are directly related to deficiencies in some vitamin or another.

However, food and nutrition instruction doesn't have to be as dull as what we experienced in high school. There are plenty of ways to encourage nutritional knowledge without turning it into a lecture.

For example, some excellent ways to incorporate food and nutrition into activities are:

- Weekly recipe raffles (Throughout the week, residents are allowed to submit recipes of their own. Then, on a specified day, one recipe is drawn and cooked by your kitchen staff.)
- Cooking classes
- Picnics
- Farmer's market visits
- Discussion groups
- Alcohol-free happy hours

And, of course, most of your partners for this activity will be food and transportation-related. For example:

- Local transportation companies
- Local schools
- Volunteer chefs from various ethnic specialties
- Local grocery stores
- Farmer's markets

Intergenerational Programs and Partnerships

Intergenerational programs are an excellent source of stimulation for both older adults and the youth partaking in them. These programs, usually conducted with high school students, help the older generations pass down cultural traditions while also encouraging sensible values amongst our youth.

To implement a program like this, we recommend reaching out to local high schools and meeting with them to see if they would be interested in offering an intergenerational program to their students. Many high schools will accept and offer the program as extra credit, an alternative to suspension/expulsion, or even a class on its own.

To further improve your odds of being able to implement a program like this, you can apply to be part of an existing program that connects youth with older adults.

Some examples of programs you can apply for include:

- AARP Foundation Experience Corps
- Generations United
- Jumpstart
- Senior Corps Foster Grandparents

For more intergenerational programs in your area, you can also visit Generations United's Intergenerational Program Database at gu.org/ig-program-database.

Chapter 15

Next Steps for the Active Investor

You have learned enough by now to know what type of Senior Living facility you want to invest in and whether you want to be an active investor in this industry. If you have decided that being an active investor is right for you, here are a few things you can do right now to get started on your journey:

- **Write down the type of Senior Living facility you want to invest in.** Just putting your idea down on paper is a commitment in itself. Now start making plans to actively invest in this area. Will you invest in RALs or something else? Will you offer memory care? Where will you invest? What type of property are you looking for? Will you do ground-up development or buy and retrofit existing buildings?

- **Start with where you are and create an action plan for the next seven days, 30 days, and 90 days.** List your goals for acquiring and operating Senior Living facilities and craft benchmarks to help you get there. Then, please do everything you can to meet those goals using the information we've discussed in this book.

- **Keep in mind that, as you determine your next steps, what you *know* is not important, but learning the industry is.** Even if you aren't sure how to reach a goal, list it. As you traverse along your journey, you'll be forced to learn more and more until you're a veritable Senior Living expert. How will you learn more? Will you go to conferences? Will you find a coaching program, mentor, or home study course? Will you invest as a passive investor in someone else's Senior Living project and have them teach you the ropes? Make a plan and stick to it.

- **Network, network, network.** In many industries– and *especially* real estate– who you know is just as important as what you know. Make it a goal to network with several commercial realtors (they can keep you keyed in on the latest market properties), real estate lawyers, and other Senior Living investors. And start talking to everyone you know who might invest with you as you develop your Senior Living business.

- **Finally**, understand that *where* you start is not important. It's that you start and stick to it. So long as you begin your journey and stick with it, you can achieve success in any business. Perseverance is key to long-term success.

We believe in you.

PART 3

HOW TO BE A PASSIVE INVESTOR

Chapter 16

Senior Living as a Passive Investment

For passive investors, your experience will be characterized by finding someone who is actively acquiring or developing Senior Living establishments. The idea is to find someone who is looking for passive investors so that you can invest with them while they do all the work, and you collect income from your cash investment as a source of passive income. Certain passive investments may give you some say in the decisions of the business but will also allow you to take on other pursuits while the day-to-day operations are handled by your investment partner(s).

Passive investment involves allowing an active investor the use of your money with the expectation that they will acquire or develop and operate a Senior Living facility in such a manner that it will yield positive returns for their passive investors in the future. It is difficult for most people to consider investing, let alone deferring money into Senior Living homes, a previously misunderstood industry.

Senior Living has gained prominence over the years as a significant housing option for older people in the residential sector. It has also become a promising form of passive investment for those willing to divert investment funds from other commercial real estate asset classes or traditional investments. There are numerous reasons why Senior Living is an excellent investment, all of which we have covered in previous chapters.

However, passively investing in Senior Living projects is not for everyone. Where with active investment, your profits are entirely dependent on your own actions, passive investment puts your financial investment in someone else's control. A well-managed investment can generate a profit, while a poorly managed investment can cost you your invested dollars.

Senior Living Syndications

We've mentioned this already, but the form of residential Senior Living investment you're looking for as a passive investor is a real estate syndication model. With syndication, a group of passive investors like yourself pool their money together with an active management team to fund the acquisition, development, and operation of a Senior Living project. The only difference between a multi-family or commercial syndicate and a Senior Living syndicate is an additional operations entity that will hire and manage staff and daily operations at the facility.

In a typical syndicate, there are two major classes of members involved in the transaction: the investor class and the management class. For a Senior Living facility, the management class is the asset manager for the real estate and either hires an independent operator or acts as the operator of the facility. Both will make their fair share of profit from the transactions, albeit in different ways.

For the operator (your role if you are an active investor), your money is paid from monthly profits, the original transaction, management fees, etc. For the investor (your compensation if you are a passive investor) is a share of monthly cash flow and a share of eventual resale profits. The amount you make is dependent on the amount you pledge initially, as well as the percentage of profit you and the sponsor agree on.

Benefits of Passive Senior Living Investing

Senior Living investment, especially in the passive form, represents a host of benefits that many never stop to consider. Here are a few that you should be aware of when deciding if passive Senior Living investing is for you:

Free Up Time and Avoid Massive Headaches

Passive Senior Living investing, and passive investing in general, is great for serial entrepreneurs who like to automate their income streams. This form of investing allows you to have a hand in important financial decisions without being responsible for day-to-day management.

With the extra time you have, you can work on other side pursuits, enjoy your retirement, or further develop your own real estate investment portfolio.

Achieve Higher Levels of Diversification

With commercial and general real estate investment, it isn't easy for a single investor who invests on their own to achieve true diversification or the level of management required for your properties. With passive investing in Senior Living homes, though, you are presented with a unique opportunity to both fund future investment efforts and achieve deeper diversification of your investment portfolio. Your investments can be spread across multiple assets, in multiple locations, and for varying durations of time so that your portfolio achieves a truly diversified outlook.

Lower Credit Risk and Fewer Liabilities

With investors, it's well-known that putting all your financial eggs into one basket is a bad idea. Being able to invest in multiple other ventures while your investment in a Senior Living facility is off generating revenue can be a blessing on its own. This way, even if one of the other investments fails, you have a safety net, as all of your investments are unlikely to fail at once.

Cash Flow

Passive real estate investing, when done correctly, can provide a reliable stream of income that requires very little management. Over time, you can use this cash flow to invest in new pursuits, increase your investment in existing ones, or even just use it to maintain your own standard of living.

Requires Limited Knowledge

Perhaps the most coveted benefit of passive Senior Living investing is that it doesn't require as much in-depth knowledge as active investment does. Where active investors may have to study and be mentored for years before finally taking on their first real estate investment property, passive Senior Living investing allows you to jump straight in with a limited working knowledge, relying on the knowledge of the syndicator to generate profit for you.

In fact, according to CBRE Senior Housing & Care Market Insight (Q1 2018), passive investors in Senior Living projects can average 12 percent or more in returns without doing any work themselves to actively manage a Senior Living project.

Furthermore, if you invest with a Senior Living syndicator, you only need a small working knowledge of Senior Living investments. Your Senior Living syndicator will manage all of the finer details, like:

- Projecting and monitoring profits and losses
- Structuring the company in a way that helps to mitigate risk to passive investors
- Addressing issues that could cost you profit, like slow construction or legal hold-ups
- Anticipating large expenses and making plans for how to manage them
- Managing bookkeeping and accounting
- Overseeing onsite personnel and resident care

Many new investors tend to underestimate the work of a Senior Living syndicator, but they do a lot of behind-the-scenes work to help make sure the facility functions and stays profitable. Meanwhile, you, as the passive investor, can sit back and enjoy effortless earnings.

Provides Passive Gains and Losses

Passive gains and losses are common when investing—after all, just about every thing you'll do as a *passive investor* will be *passive.* Writing these types of gains and losses off on your taxes can be extremely advantageous.

For example, let's say you sign a deal, and the first year the deal is operational, you only experience losses. This happens for many reasons; perhaps there's no cash flow yet while the property is being readied for occupancy, or it's a development project that is still undergoing construction. Whatever the reason, your deal may lose money in the beginning year or two of operations.

These losses usually aren't long-term but can still be written off on your taxes. They may be able to be deducted from your tax bill, resulting in larger gains from other projects because you're paying fewer overall taxes.

Encourages Social Responsibility

As a passive investor, you won't have a direct hand in helping your senior residents manage their lives or in keeping them entertained and happy. However, you will have a direct hand in providing them with the environment they need to thrive, and you can feel good about that.

We've laid out the demographics in previous chapters, and they aren't lying. The number of seniors who will need Senior Living housing is rising much more rapidly than the number of housing facilities available to them. By investing, you can help mitigate this shortage and make a positive social impact.

Senior Living housing has the potential to outperform all other real estate investment classes, but that isn't the only reason you should consider investing in Senior Living facilities. The eight reasons above (among many, many others) make it well worth it to invest in Senior Living as a passive real estate venture.

Chapter 17

Understanding Your Investment

While passive investment requires significantly less effort than active investment, that doesn't mean you can skip out on doing your research. It's crucial that you take the time to understand the parameters and implications of your investment and the asset class you are investing in.

In traditional investments, such as the stock market, the parameters are simple. You invest your money and take it out when you want to, pay taxes on your earnings, and pay any fees you're expected to pay. With real estate and Senior Living deals, though, there may be different expectations and rules. You'll have a different set of projected returns, different amounts of equity, and new tax implications. Most real estate and Senior Living investments are non-liquid, meaning you are expected to stay invested for the period of time your syndicate owns the property, which could be indefinite due to market fluctuations, etc.

For this, we emphasize that you should take the time to do the leg work, and research, *research, **research,*** which should include learning about the syndicator, the proposed management team, and their track records with similar properties.

Getting Paid

The biggest question in any deal (and likely the reason you're reading this book today) is how much you can get paid and *when* if you are a passive investor in a Senior Living facility. And while we can't say exactly when this will be because we have no way of knowing what deal you'll be getting into, we do have some information on how you can find out for yourself.

Whenever you invest money in a real estate deal as a passive investor, you are issued what is called a PPM (Private Placement Memorandum).

This document is a single, comprehensive outline that covers all the details surrounding the financial offering.

The PPM you receive will outline all the various aspects of your deal, such as:

- How long can you expect your capital to be tied up in the project (usually a minimum of 3 years); but could be as long as 7-10 years. Make sure to look the projected timeframe up in the PPM and ensure that it matches the timeline for when you want to get your money back.
- Any syndication management fees that will be taken out before profit is determined.
- Projected annualized returns on your investment. This is calculated by adding the projected cash flow returns plus projected returns (over and above your return of capital) from the eventual sale or refinance of the project; then dividing the sum of these numbers by the number of years your funds were invested. Divide the resulting amount by the amount of your original investment and convert it to a percentage to determine your annualized percentage return on investment.
- Any other specific terms your deal requires.

It is important to note as well that a PPM is not like the business plan used by active investors. It doesn't provide any sort of persuasive content because it is only issued once a deal has already begun. Instead, it provides the investor with crucial information relevant to their investment decision.

The PPM should present information to the investor in a non-biased and factual manner. It should point out the potential gains as well as address the risks associated with the investment. Past that, it should include accurate and up-to-date information on the property, your plan of operations for it, and the management team executing the investment plan.

In general, the PPM you receive should have the following points, among others:

- Introduction
- Terms summary
- Risk factors
- Company description
- Management team overview
- Use of proceeds
- Description of securities
- Subscription procedures
- Exhibits with information about the property, including the syndicator's sources and uses of funds, projected year-by-year cash flow, and proposed exit strategy for the property and for investors.

Additionally, some deals will offer a single return-on-investment (ROI) method (such as a fixed return for a finite duration versus a share of cash flow and equity on sale), while others may give you choices or allow you to participate in several different methods concurrently.

The following are some common forms of ROI you may see as a Senior Living investor.

Preferred Returns

Preferred returns are distributed either monthly or quarterly once the project has begun to generate cash flow. Preferred returns may just offer a predetermined, fixed-rate that doesn't change once it has been established, or they may include a profit-sharing component.

The reason this investment return type is called "preferred" is that if you are part of a "preferred class" of investors, you generally receive your

ROI before the other classes of members of a syndicate.

Profit Sharing or Equity Participation

Profit sharing is a type of ROI that provides the investor with an opportunity to share in the project's profits. This gives the investor (you) the opportunity to make more money if the project does well. Very typically, investors in a syndicate will be offered a preferred return from cash flow plus a share of profits after the management team has taken a cut.

Additionally, profits can be generated from resale. The idea is that the syndicator will improve or develop the property, get it fully occupied, operate it for a period of time at maximum capacity to maximize the property's value, and then eventually sell it to a new buyer or refinance it after the value has increased.

The difference between the sale price and liabilities (such as outstanding loans or expenses) is called "equity." The proceeds from the sale (or a cash-out refinance) are first used to pay off liabilities of the company, then return the investors' capital contributions, then make arrearages in preferred returns from cash flow, give the syndicator its cut, and the remainder is generally split between investors and the syndicate management team. This is where wealth is generated.

There *are* benefits to this type of return on investment. While your ultimate returns may be fully dependent on how well the project does, it also allows you, as the investor, to enjoy tax deductions associated with passive losses during the early years of operations before cash flow is generated and while improvements are being made.

These types of losses can make for excellent tax deductions later, and some may be carried forward to future years, so be sure to discuss this with your CPA or tax attorney.

Fixed Return

A fixed return offering is a lot like preferred returns in that you are paid out a predetermined amount of money each month. Again, like preferred returns, this is one of the lowest-risk ROI methods because you may receive payouts regardless of the project's financial standing. Because of this, though, the amount offered is usually lower than other ROI offerings. Once a fixed-return investor is paid back its original capital contribution plus the fixed return owed, it usually relinquishes its interests and is no longer part of the deal.

This is not to say that fixed income ROI is bad, though. For some people, it represents the perfect balance of return on investment and low risk. It is ideal for those who want a reliable source of passive income. It's also great for those seeking out new methods of income without complicating their tax filings.

There is one major aspect of receiving money from your passive real estate investment you shouldn't forget to consider, though: risk management.

No matter how good a deal may sound, there is always the chance the investment will fail. If this happens, you could very well lose the money you've put into it. That's part of the risk you take when you want to incur major returns.

Admittedly, with Senior Living investing, the chances of this happening are slimmer than with other types of real estate deals because of the supply and demand factors we mentioned in Part 1 of this book. However, that doesn't mean it can't or won't happen.

What Happens If A Senior Living Facility You Invested In Fails?

As you may have suspected, there's a process. With all real estate, the underlying assets (i.e., the building and the land it's built on) have some underlying value. So, if the investment were to fail, the building and land could be sold to recover some of the funds invested in the project. Any debts or liens would have to be satisfied first (including any outstanding loan balances, property taxes, contractors, etc.), and any remaining funds would be distributed to investors based on their respective priority rights.

It is important to understand that a major part of your job as an investor is to limit the potential of investment loss by vetting the syndicate management teams, conducting proper research, and investigating any questionable aspects of a project, such as wildly speculative projections, etc. You should never enter a real estate deal of any kind without first asking questions and satisfying yourself that the management team has the right experience, the projections are conservative, and the results of the project feasibility study are sound.

Even the most passive investments require some commitment on your end. Your responsibility is to choose the investments that you feel have the best opportunity to succeed—and to ensure you trust the management team and operators heading the deal.

This responsibility will *always* rest on your shoulders. Even if you hire someone to scout out the Senior Living deal for you, the burden of deciding will always come back to you, as the consequences of choosing the wrong offering will ultimately impact you in the end.

Building Your Pre-Investment Toolkit

With investing, giving a bright-eyed prospect your money and hoping for the best is simply not enough— even with how reliable the Senior Living market is. As such, there are a few things you want to make sure you do before *every single investment*. We call these things your **pre-investment toolkit.**

The Following Tools and Strategies Should be in Your Toolkit:

Know Your Operators

The best indicator of whether a project will be successful is the operator. No matter how good a business plan or foundation a Senior Living facility has, it will fail under the wrong leadership.

In fact, for *any* real estate deal, the success of the investment is almost entirely dependent on the operator and management team's ability to market the offering and manage the project.

As such, you should always investigate your operator and management team before agreeing to pledge money toward a project. If you don't trust the team in charge of your money, there's a good chance you'll end up getting burned.

Prioritize Transparency

You should always choose deals where transparent communication takes precedence over potential profits. In fact, any deal that advertises higher-than-average profits while attempting to obscure the details of your deal should be immediately cast aside. These will end up being money-pits at best and highly illegal at worst.

The best way to ensure communication is prioritized is to have a discussion with the investment manager. Ask questions regarding their availability if you have a question or concern, and observe how they communicate with you in the meantime.

Some questions to ask yourself are: What's their average response time? Are they thorough in answering your questions? Have you caught them attempting to conceal information? What past projects have they been a part of? How did these projects pan out?

If you're able to, always ask for references before entering a deal. This will help you get a solid idea of how your project manager operates in the beginning, middle, and end stages of an offering.

You should also check the LinkedIn profiles of the professionals on the management team. Verify their credentials and get a written statement that property updates will be provided regularly, even if just over email. Because Senior Living is such a lucrative market right now, a lot of new operators on jumping on board. You don't want your money tied up in their experiment—*especially since many of them likely have not read this book.*

Know The Market

Without adequate information on the market, it is going to be difficult to choose a reliable offering to sink your money into. This book already serves as a solid foundation for your Senior Living market knowledge, but real estate is ever-changing. There will always be more to learn, and those new concepts could end up affecting your investment.

Diversify Your Portfolio

Anyone who has put even an ounce of effort into developing a portfolio knows that the cardinal rule of investment is to diversify. The reason for this comes down to risk. Senior Living as an industry is more reliable than most others. However, that doesn't mean its security is guaranteed. And if something *does* happen, and you've stacked all your eggs in a single basket, you may not be able to recover from it.

As such, any investment partners you take on should understand the importance of diversification. If you find a syndicator is pressuring you to invest in a deal, be cautious. The best syndicators have more investors than opportunities, and they won't pressure you to invest if you are uncertain. Investing in private offerings isn't for everyone. If you are afraid you are going to be nervous about your investment, it might not be a good fit. You might be better off with traditional investments.

Also, never invest more than you could recover from if it ends up being a total loss. Also, don't invest if you are depending on the income to sustain your lifestyle, such as a mortgage, car payment, etc. A syndicator may need to suspend distributions during times of crisis, like COVID-19, or a catastrophic event at the property, such as a fire.

There's no doubt that passive investments can ultimately generate success—but that doesn't mean you should flip a coin, close your eyes, and wait to see how it lands. Passive investments require due diligence by the investor, and an investor who doesn't realize this may have failed before he/she has started.

You shouldn't take a deal just because the label "Senior Living" or "Residential Assisted Living (RAL)" is slapped along the top. It would be best if you did your homework, put in the time, investigate the background and experience of the management team and the property, and never stop learning.

The more knowledge you have, the more power you have to create your own success.

Invest from Within

Over the course of your investment career, you will encounter many things. You'll make investments of time, money, and energy that don't always pay out. You'll invest in industries you never thought you would, and you may have investment opportunities you *love* that never make it into your portfolio.

You may never even end up putting money into the Senior Living industry. And that's okay.

Much of the investment advice in this book can be applied across a range of real estate investments, not just Senior Living. So long as you apply these principles where you can, you can have many successful investments in your lifetime.

Some, however, will fail. This is an important thing to realize.

No matter how much work you put in or how much homework you do, the world of investing is volatile and unpredictable. There will be factors in play that you can't control, and events will happen that you can't predict. There will be times when you lack self-confidence, times when you procrastinate, and the opportunity goes away, and times when you just make a bad call. When it happens, it can be a major blow to your confidence. It will cause a stir of negative emotions, and you may have trouble recovering from it. But you will recover.

You may need a little trial and error to figure out if you're better suited for active or passive investment. For some people, the distinction is obvious. Active investors know they'd rather be the ones putting the shovel in the ground, digging up the dirt, putting the mortar on the bricks, and slapping them together. Passive investors know they want to play around behind the scenes and manage multiple investments at once.

For others, however, the distinction is not so easy. There are factors in both classes that appeal to them. They aren't sure what would fit their personality better and must experiment to reach a final decision. There's also always the chance that an investor thinks he/she is best suited for one role when really, they excel in the other. Many active investors start out investing passively just to learn the ropes. After a time, they believe they can do it themselves and decide to try an active role.

In short, you never *really* know what's best for you until you put your nose to the grindstone and find out.

For these reasons, we've tried to share our collective knowledge on both active and passive investment types, as well as the opportunities presented through Senior Living development projects. Through our experience investing in RAL and Senior Living communities, we've come to realize that there are opportunities here for every investor. It's up to you to decide which ones are right for you.

Marco Pierre White said, "I think self-discovery is the greatest achievement in life because once you discover yourself and accept what you are, then you can fulfill your true potential and be happy."

And how right he was. Life is all about discovering who you are; the older you become, the more experiences you have. The more experiences you have, the more you come to know yourself.

Now, we hope you're really paying attention to this part. We're about to give you some advice that takes most people years to discover on their own. In fact, some people never discover it at all.

Are you ready?

Here it is:

At the end of the day, money is money.

It's true. You can live every day putting your entire efforts into increasing the amounts in your bank account. And yet, at the end of your career, you will still find yourself lacking something.

Too often, investment is treated as an end and not the means to an end. It's used as a method to make money, nothing more. It doesn't have to be that way, though.

Being able to serve various communities, maintain integrity, and use your talents to help others live a better quality of life introduces a whole new aspect to investing. It gives your actions meaning. Suddenly, your wins are more than just wins for you; they're wins for the seniors and staff members you're helping. There is a win in every Senior Living in a housing project you helped build. There is a win for every resident's family member who can now rest easier at night knowing their beloved seniors are safely housed because of the service you provide.

Chapter 18

What Type of Investor Are You?

Before you begin reading this section, you should know that it is interactive. We'll be walking you through developing a rudimentary understanding of what type of investor you are, and you'll be asked to write some things down.

On the pages following, there will be space for you to answer the questions we ask if you wish to write directly in the book. If you don't want to do that, a piece of paperwork is just as well. You can even grab your laptop and type out your answers if you wish. Then, you'll have a copy you can print and add as the first page of your new investment binder—or frame to put up on your wall!

Take a moment now to gather any of the above materials you'll need. Once you have them, begin reading and filling out the information below.

#1: Risk Tolerance

You're likely aware by now of the risks investing can present. Every new investment opportunity comes with a unique set of risks and rewards, and it's up to you to determine whether one outweighs the other and how much risk you're willing to take.

We call this your risk/reward threshold.

Naturally, greater risk exposes you to greater losses—but it also allows you to ascertain greater rewards. The safer you play, the less you stand to gain. For example, putting your savings in the bank is a safe way to gain interest on it, but you aren't going to get, say, a 10% ROI doing that, are you?

Senior Living investment is great in this respect. The industry consistently yields rewards year after year, as it has for nearly a decade. Even those with extremely low-risk profiles are usually able to find a deal that suits their needs.

If you don't know what your threshold is, don't worry. That's what this section is for.

You can think of the risk/reward threshold as a line ranging from 1 to 10. The more willing you are to risk your capital, the higher on the scale your portfolio should be placed.

For reference, "1" is the lowest. People at this point in the scale are not willing to take any risk with their capital. They are considered **conservative** with their investments. In fact, they may be uncomfortable just putting their money in the bank because of the possibility of a bank run.

On the other side of the scale, "10" is the highest. Investors who reside here are considered the most **speculative.** These people are the types of investors who are willing to put it all on the line for a gamble. They know and are comfortable with the fact that they might lose all their money at any given time. It doesn't bother them because they know they also stand to gain the most and feel confident they can recover from a loss if and when it happens.

On the line below, take a moment to jot down an indication of where you believe you fall on this scale.

Conservative ➡ Speculative

1 ——————————————— 10

As you decide where you fall, remember both extremely conservative and extremely speculative people exist. Neither is better or worse than the other, nor are they necessarily better or worse than any other point on the scale. It all depends on how you build your portfolio around that preference.

#2: Level of Sophistication

No, we aren't talking about the typical, high-class type of sophistication. Rather, we're talking about sophistication in an investment context. In other words, your financial sophistication.

Financial sophistication refers to how knowledgeable you are when it comes to investments. Do you understand the potential values and potential pitfalls of the investments you're looking into? Do you know how to balance those things to determine whether you're making the right decision? Do you understand how to mitigate risk in a high-risk deal to better suit your portfolio?

Your answers to each of these questions indicate your level of financial sophistication.

It is always better to be more financially sophisticated because it indicates that you are more well-informed. However, you should not lie to yourself and tell yourself you are more knowledgeable than you are—especially here.

No one is here to watch or judge your answers, and it is important that you tell yourself the truth so you know where you stand among other investors. This will help you understand how much more knowledge you should seek out before making your first major investment.

On the line below, indicate where you believe you reside on the scale of financial sophistication. A "1" in this contest indicates that this book is the first investment-oriented piece of literature you've read. You may not have understood a lot of the jargon, and you may have had to keep Google open as you thumbed through it.

"10," on the other hand, indicates that you knew the principles in this book before we taught them to you. The knowledge here is nothing new, and you mostly read this book to gauge the state of the Senior Living industry before making an investment.

Most people reading this book will fall somewhere in the middle, but it is not impossible to have some of you mark yourselves as one of the two extremes.

Non-Sophisticated ➡ Sophisticated

1 —————————————————— 10

#3: Sacrifice

When most people here "sacrifice" for the first time as it pertains to investment, they assume it has something to do with that risk/reward scale we examined above. However, that's not what we're referring to here.

Instead, what we're discussing here refers to your willingness to sacrifice life's basics (such as time, money, or comfort) to reach your goals. If you want to be a successful investor in RAL or active Senior Living housing, you'll need to be comfortable with a certain degree of sacrifice.

It is also important to realize that some of you reading this book will be **willing** to sacrifice time, money, or comfort but not **able** to. Maybe you're ready to put those things on the line, but you don't yet have the footing to be able to—and that's okay!

www.VinneyChopra.com/FreeBenefits

Every person who has ever been successful has started somewhere. The thing that separates those who have found success from those who haven't are having two intrinsic qualities: ambition and resourcefulness.

You must know how to get what you don't have, and if you don't know how to get it, you must be willing to figure it out. You'll have to work to be an optimist and see life as an opportunity rather than an obstacle.

Remember: when was the last time you saw a successful person who blamed the world around them for their shortcomings?

Never!

Success tends to avoid those who are pessimists in life. If you want to attract good deals and great allies, you need to put out that positive energy.

Now, that said, let's get on to the next scale.

In this section, you'll indicate how willing you are to make sacrifices. You will rank the following items # 1, 2, or 3, depending on how willing you are to sacrifice them:

1. Time
2. Comfort
3. Money

In the following table, on Line #1, using the three choices above, write the thing that you are most willing to sacrifice. On-Line #2, write the thing you are second most willing to sacrifice, and on Line #3, write the thing you are least willing to sacrifice.

Conservative ➡ Sacrificial

1.

2.	
3.	

The purpose of this exercise is to tell you what kind of Senior Living, whether active or passive investment, is going to be best for you. The answers you put in the three lines above will help you better understand your position. Those who noted that they are most inclined to sacrifice time or comfort first tend to excel at active investing, while those who are most comfortable with sacrificing money tend to be passive investors.

There is, however, a chance that you got a mixture of both results. Perhaps you noted that you are most willing to sacrifice money. In that case, it indicates that you have a high-risk tolerance and may find yourself investing in deals with higher potential rewards.

#4: Terms of Investment

We've covered several different types of investment terms in this book. Generally, these will be noted in the PPM you receive when you are offered a deal. However, PPMs contain a great deal of information, so it's always best to know what you're looking for before you open that packet for the first time.

For example, private placements offer a specific length of time that your money will be tied up in the deal. Usually, this is anywhere from 2 to 7 years, though it can be shorter or longer under certain circumstances.

With investing, the longer your money is tied up in a deal, the more money you'll generally make. As such, investors who are secure in believing a deal will succeed will try to push for a longer term to increase their returns.

Long-term investments are great for those who don't want to go through the trouble of having to reinvest every few years. Instead, you can keep your money cycling through the project and gain passive revenue as it is gradually paid back to you. This will decrease the amount of time you must sacrifice.

Keeping your money "active" like this is the core of investing like a pro. If your money isn't actively making you *more money,* then you might as well be losing it. However, it does take a significant amount of time and work to keep money deployed securely. As such, once you're lucky enough to find a deal with the right terms and a team/operator you trust, you should work to build those relationships so you can keep your money working.

For this section, we don't have a scale as much as we do a set of questions for you to answer. These questions will help you understand what to look for in a PPM or project proposal. By answering them to the best of your ability, you'll help mitigate that feeling of being overwhelmed when your first deal lands in your lap.

When you're ready, answer the questions below:

- ✓ How long are you reasonably willing and able to keep your money committed to one project?

- ✓ Would you rather invest in assets you can sell quickly (more liquid) or assets that are slower to sell but hold more value (less liquid)?

- ✓ Do you prefer to invest with companies whose management team you are familiar with, or are you willing to take a chance on someone new?

- ✓ What types of returns do you prefer? Would you rather have a lump sum or a monthly or quarterly distribution?

By answering these questions, you'll already know how to react when you are approached by a syndicator or first open your PPM. You'll understand which terms will work with your preferences versus which ones will work against them.

There are, of course, many other terms that will be included in your PPM, but these questions are foundational – if the terms being offered don't match your investing goals, then you shouldn't make that investment. For example, if you aren't willing to work with a team you aren't already familiar with, you'll save yourself a lot of time by flipping through the team section first. If you don't want to be in a ten-year deal, then flip to the section about the duration of the investment. If you want to achieve a specific return, then look for the syndicator's projections and determine whether you think they are based on reasonable assumptions – and if you don't believe their projections are achievable, don't invest.

By priming your brain to make these decisions, you'll be better able to decide whether to go ahead or decide you don't want to proceed any further.

#5: Investment Goal

The next question you should know your position on involves the overall goal of why you're investing in the first place. Some people invest because they want or need an extra income stream. Some people invest because they like the tax benefits. Others still invest because they enjoy the research or risk that investing provides.

All of these are great reasons, and both active and passive forms of investment can provide these things. However, depending on what your goal is, either active or passive investment may not be the best option for you.

That's what this section is all about. As an investor, your job is to know what goals you're working towards, why you're working towards them, and how you can make them come to fruition.

For example, if your goal was to generate several different passive income streams to eventually replace your normal 9 to 5 job, then you'd want to seek out a passive investment opportunity where you can elect for regular payouts, such as those that you'd get from preferred returns rather than end of project profit sharing.

So, what's your "why"?

On the lines below, note the top three reasons you're considering investing in Senior Living projects.

1.	
2.	
3.	

Remember, there's no right or wrong answer here. Your "why" is something that matters only to you. Even if it's as simple as saying, "I want to be rich," that's a perfectly valid reason. Just make sure you adapt your investment strategy to support that goal.

#6: Investment Level

Investment level pertains to how much you're willing to invest in general, as well as how much you're willing to invest right now. Certain passive investments allow entry at just $25,000 or $50,000 in certain instances. Active investing, however, usually costs quite a bit more.

Keep in mind, though, that active investing does not have to involve only your money. With active investing, you gain the ability to ask others to invest in your project, effectively lowering the financial threshold that you must cover on your own.

On the scale below, indicate how much you're willing and able to invest, from $100 to $1,000,000. This will give you a good idea of your current financial standing and whether you need to obtain a better source of funds or bring on other management-level partners with money before you start moving toward actively seeking a Senior Living investment.

It is important to realize that these numbers represent two extremes, as with all of our scales. Most people will have more or less than these amounts, but it is also okay if you lie on one of these extremes! All we are doing is helping you grasp your current position and ability to invest.

$100 ➡ $1,000,000

1 ——————————————— 10

This scale is made for people who have a vague idea of how much they can spend but not quite an exact number. If you *do* have an exact number, feel free to write it underneath the line.

#7: Team

You'll never see the most successful investors working alone. This principle is showcased even in this book, with myself being a syndicator in over 40+ syndicated investments; I have partners and team members who invest in multifamily, hotels, startups, and Senior Living real estate and work to support one other in our many ventures.

By creating or being part of a team, you open yourself up to new opportunities and gain the ability to leverage each other's strengths.

Most commonly, you'll see teams that tend to stick together with active RAL and Senior Living investing. This is because people tend to network with those who complement their own skills, and active investing demands a diverse group of people with complementary skills who work well together.

However, this does not mean that a team is not needed for passive investing. At the very least, you should have (or network with) a financial advisor, lawyer, and tax advisor. I recommend going further than that, though, and joining forces with one or two people you absolutely trust.

If you don't have a team in mind yet, don't worry. It can take a few years in the field before your ideal team comes together. Though, that doesn't mean you can't get a jump on the process.

On the lines below, take a moment to write down three people you would consider teaming up with. This can be three people you know personally, individuals in the industry you admire, or a combination of both.

1.	
2.	
3.	

Depending on who you are, you may not have three people to write down, and that's fine too. If this is the case, you can always join online forums, stock investment clubs, or network at a meet-and-greet or Senior Living events.

#8: Tax Strategy

With investment, taxes take on a different form than the typical W-2 forms that most people see. For some investors, understanding the tax structure is a major obstacle to their success. For others, the tax benefits investing provides are a large part of the reason they enter the industry in the first place.

As such, every investor has different tax plans. Some use investment as an opportunity to dodge capital gains taxes and continuously defer them. Some will try to simplify tax season for themselves by identifying the easiest return to file and following the instructions to the letter.

Whichever method you choose will largely depend on your level of knowledge.

Naturally, the higher the difficulty you are willing to partake in when filing your taxes, the more benefits you're able to derive. On the line below, indicate what level of difficulty you're willing to take on with your tax situation.

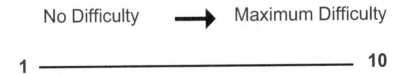

No Difficulty ➡ Maximum Difficulty

1 ———————————————— 10

Your choice will affect what sort of professional help you need to seek out. For those who want the least amount of difficulty possible, you'll simply want to find a tax professional when tax season rolls around and have them file your tax returns for you. You may even be able to take your information and file it yourself, depending on your level of knowledge.

For those who are okay with as much difficulty as possible so long as it saves them money, your needs will be very different. You'll need to seek out a specialized tax expert do to your filings, and it's recommended that you maintain regular contact with them throughout the fiscal year as you make new investments. You'll also need to work together one-on-one with your tax expert to develop a plan and a set of expectations.

As you seek out someone to help with your taxes, though, be aware that different tax advisors will have different levels of experience. You'll want to work with one who is experienced in both tax preparation **and** tax strategy for real estate investors. You may have to vet several before you find one that is right for you.

Trust Yourself

By this point, you should have a decent grasp of what type of investor you are, what you prefer, and whether an active or passive style is more your speed. However, none of this means anything unless you learn to trust yourself.

As you begin to explore the Senior Living community, there will be people who wholeheartedly support you. There will be others who try to convince you that what you're doing isn't right and that you should be doing things a different way. This may or may not be true, and it's up to you to figure that out. But you shouldn't ever change the way you do things just because other people tell you to.

If someone offers a suggestion, explore it, and give it a chance. If you ultimately decide it isn't right for you, stick by that.

And remember: no matter what path you choose, our team, which includes Vinney Chopra, Shahid Imran, and Jon Roosen, will be here to help you along the way.

We can't wait to help you begin your Senior Living investment journey.

PART 4

CASE STUDIES

Chapter 19

My Senior Living Projects

Premier MONEIL Senior Communities

I will start first with 8-16 units RAL Facility:

Building a profitable Residential Assisted Living (RAL) business from scratch involves several key steps. Here is a detailed breakdown of the process:

1. *Research and Planning*:

   a. Conduct market research to identify the demand for RAL services in your target location.

   b. Analyze the local demographic trends, competition, and regulatory requirements.

   c. Develop a comprehensive business plan outlining your vision, goals, target market, financial projections, and marketing strategies.

2. *Secure Funding*:

   a. Determine the financial requirements for starting and operating your RAL business.

   b. Explore funding options such as personal savings, loans, partnerships, or investment opportunities.

   c. Prepare a detailed financial proposal and seek financing from lenders or investors.

3. *Identify Suitable Location*:

   a. Look for a location that meets zoning and regulatory requirements for operating a RAL facility.

b. Consider factors such as accessibility, proximity to healthcare facilities, amenities, and a supportive community environment.

c. Research local real estate options and consult with a commercial real estate agent to find a suitable property.

4. *Licensing and Compliance:*

a. Research and understand the licensing and regulatory requirements for operating a RAL facility in your area.

b. Contact the relevant regulatory agencies to obtain the necessary licenses and permits.

c. Develop policies and procedures that align with regulatory standards, including resident care, safety protocols, staffing requirements, and record keeping.

5. *Facility Design and Construction:*

a. Engage architects and contractors experienced in building RAL facilities.

b. Develop a functional and aesthetically pleasing facility design that meets the needs of residents.

c. Ensure compliance with accessibility guidelines, safety codes, and fire regulations.

6. *Staffing and Training:*

a. Hire a competent team, including administrators, nurses, caregivers, activity coordinators, and support staff.

b. Conduct thorough background checks and ensure all staff members meet the necessary qualifications and training requirements.

c. Provide ongoing training and professional development opportunities to enhance the quality of care and services.

7. *Establish Relationships with Healthcare Providers:*

a. Establish partnerships with local healthcare providers, such as doctors, hospitals, and pharmacies.

b. Collaborate with professionals in geriatric care, therapy services, and other relevant specialties to offer comprehensive care to residents.

c. Develop referral networks to attract potential residents and build credibility within the healthcare community.

8. *Marketing and Promotion:*

a. Develop a marketing strategy to promote your RAL business to potential residents and their families.

b. Create a strong brand identity and online presence through a professional website, social media, and online directories.

c. Utilize traditional marketing methods, such as print materials, local events, and community outreach initiatives, to raise awareness.

9. *Operational Management:*

a. Implement efficient operational processes to ensure smooth day-to-day operations.

b. Develop resident care plans, medication management systems, and procedures for emergencies and safety.

c. Continuously monitor and evaluate operational performance, addressing any issues promptly.

10. *Continuous Improvement and Adaptation:*

a. Stay updated on industry trends, research, and best practices in senior care.

b. Seek feedback from residents, their families, and staff to identify areas for improvement.

c. Regularly assess and adapt your services, amenities, and marketing strategies to meet changing market demands and resident needs.

To increase the likelihood of success for your Residential Assisted Living (RAL) facility, consider the following strategies:

1. Thorough Market Research: Conduct comprehensive market research to understand the demand for senior care in your area. Identify the demographics, preferences, and specific needs of your target market. This information will help you tailor your services and marketing efforts accordingly.

2. Develop a Strong Business Plan: Create a detailed business plan that outlines your goals, target market, marketing strategies, financial projections, and operational plans. This plan will serve as a roadmap for your facility's success and guide your decision-making process.

3. Provide Top-Quality Care: The quality of care you provide is crucial to the success of your RAL facility. Ensure your staff members are well-trained, compassionate, and capable of meeting the unique needs of senior residents. Establish protocols for medication management, healthcare services, and emergency response to ensure the well-being of your residents.

4. Prioritize Staffing and Training: Invest in recruiting and retaining competent staff members who are passionate about senior care. Offer ongoing training and professional development opportunities to enhance their skills and knowledge. Maintaining a positive work environment and fostering a sense of teamwork can also contribute to staff satisfaction and retention.

5. Create a Safe and Comfortable Environment: Ensure your facility meets all safety standards and regulations. Implement safety features

such as handrails, non-slip flooring, and emergency call systems. Create a comfortable and homelike atmosphere by providing well-designed living spaces, communal areas, and outdoor spaces.

6. Emphasize Personalized Services: Tailor your services to meet the individual needs and preferences of your residents. Offer personalized care plans, social activities, and meal options. Encourage family involvement and communication to create a sense of community and promote resident satisfaction.

7. Effective Marketing and Networking: Develop a strong marketing strategy to raise awareness about your RAL facility. Utilize online and offline marketing channels, such as a website, social media, local events, and partnerships with healthcare professionals, community organizations, and senior centers. Maintain a positive online reputation through reviews and testimonials.

8. Maintain Financial Stability: Establish a sound financial management system to ensure the long-term sustainability of your RAL facility. Monitor expenses closely, regularly review financial reports, and adapt your operations as needed. Explore multiple revenue streams, including private pay, long-term care insurance, and potential partnerships with healthcare providers.

9. Stay Informed and Adapt: Keep abreast of industry trends, regulatory changes, and best practices in senior care. Attend conferences, join professional associations, and network with other RAL owners to stay informed and continually improve your services. Be open to adapting your business model and operations to meet evolving market needs.

10. Prioritize Resident Satisfaction: Focus on resident satisfaction and regularly seek feedback from residents, families, and staff. Address concerns promptly, implement improvement measures, and consistently strive for excellence in care provision.

Remember that success may take time and require ongoing effort. Building a strong reputation, fostering positive relationships within the community, and providing exceptional care are key factors in ensuring the success of your RAL facility.

I also want to discuss the Pitfalls here about owning a RAL.

While owning a Residential Assisted Living (RAL) facility can be a rewarding venture, it's important to be aware of the potential pitfalls and challenges that may arise. Here are some common pitfalls to consider:

1. Regulatory Compliance: RAL facilities are subject to numerous regulations and licensing requirements, which may vary by state and locality. Staying up to date with these regulations and ensuring compliance can be complex and time-consuming.

2. Staffing and Training: Hiring and retaining qualified staff members can be a challenge in the senior care industry. Finding caregivers and healthcare professionals with the right skills, experience, and compassion may require ongoing effort and investment in recruitment and training.

3. Operational Costs: Operating a RAL facility can involve significant expenses, including property maintenance, utilities, insurance, staffing costs, food, and healthcare supplies. Balancing these costs with revenue generation can be a financial challenge.

4. Resident Recruitment and Retention: Attracting and retaining residents is essential for the success of a RAL facility. Competition in the senior care industry can be fierce, and it may require effective marketing strategies and exceptional services to maintain high occupancy rates.

5. Changing Demographics and Market Trends: The senior care industry is subject to changing demographics and market trends. Keeping up with

evolving preferences, expectations, and demands of the target market can be crucial for long-term success.

6. Liability and Risk Management: Running an RAL facility comes with inherent risks, including the potential for accidents, injuries, and medical emergencies. Implementing proper risk management strategies and having comprehensive liability insurance are essential to protect yourself and your business.

7. Staff Burnout and Turnover: The demanding nature of senior care can contribute to staff burnout and high turnover rates. Providing support, training, and a positive work environment can help mitigate these challenges.

8. Evolving Healthcare Policies: Healthcare policies and regulations can change over time, impacting the operations and reimbursement structures for senior care facilities. Staying informed about policy changes and adapting your operations accordingly is crucial.

9. Reputation Management: Reputation plays a significant role in attracting residents and building trust within the community. Negative incidents, such as allegations of neglect or mistreatment, can severely impact your facility's reputation. Maintaining high-quality care and promptly addressing any concerns is essential to protect your reputation.

10. Emotional and Psychological Challenges: Working in the senior care industry can be emotionally demanding. Witnessing the decline of residents' health or dealing with end-of-life situations can take a toll on caregivers and facility owners. It's important to provide support systems and self-care strategies for yourself and your staff.

While these pitfalls should be considered, they can be managed with proper planning, continuous education, and a commitment to providing excellent care. Thoroughly researching the industry, seeking professional advice, and developing a comprehensive business plan can help you navigate these challenges effectively.

Converting a large home into a Residential Assisted Living (RAL) facility to provide top-quality service to seniors involves several steps and considerations. It's important to ensure you comply with local regulations and provide a safe and comfortable environment for your residents. Here's a general outline of the procedures and steps you might need to take:

1. Research and Planning:

 - Conduct market research to determine the demand for senior care facilities in your area.

 - Develop a detailed business plan outlining your goals, target market, services provided, staffing, and financial projections.

2. Identify the Right Property:

 - Look for a suitable large home that meets the zoning requirements for a RAL facility. Ensure it has enough space to accommodate the number of residents you plan to have.

3. Financing:

 - Secure funding for the purchase of the property and the necessary renovations/conversions. This may involve personal savings, loans, or investors.

4. Legal Structure and Licensing:

 - Decide on the legal structure for your business, such as a sole proprietorship, LLC, or corporation.

 - Obtain the required licenses and permits to operate a RAL facility in your state and local jurisdiction. Licensing requirements may vary, so be sure to check with your state's health department or licensing agency.

5. Regulatory Compliance:

- Familiarize yourself with all relevant regulations and guidelines for running a RAL facility, including safety standards, staffing requirements, and health protocols.

6. Renovation and Adaptation:

- Modify the property to meet the needs of elderly residents. This may involve installing wheelchair ramps, grab bars, wider doorways, and other accessibility features.

- Ensure the property adheres to safety codes and fire regulations.

7. Staffing and Training:

- Hire qualified staff to provide top-quality care to seniors, including caregivers, nurses, and administrative personnel.

- Ensure all staff members receive the necessary training in elder care and safety protocols.

8. Services and Amenities:

- Plan the services and amenities you will offer to residents, such as meals, medication management, recreational activities, and transportation.

9. Marketing and Admission:

- Develop a marketing strategy to attract potential residents and their families.

- Set up an admissions process to assess the needs and suitability of potential residents.

10. Launch and Ongoing Operations:

- Once all the preparations are complete, officially launch your RAL facility.

- Regularly monitor and assess the quality of care and services provided to ensure compliance with regulations and maintain top-quality service.

Remember that this is a general outline, and the specific steps and procedures may vary depending on your location and local regulations. It's crucial to consult with legal and regulatory experts and seek professional advice to ensure you are fully compliant with all applicable laws and regulations when establishing your RAL facility.

To build a profitable, premier independent, assisted senior living community with memory care and top-of-the-line amenities in a premium retirement community, consider the following steps:

1. Market Research and Feasibility Study:

a. Conduct market research to identify the demand and potential profitability of a senior living community in the desired location.

b. Evaluate the demographics, competition, and projected growth of the target market.

c. Conduct a feasibility study to assess the financial viability and potential return on investment.

2. Location Selection:

a. Identify a premium retirement community with desirable characteristics such as a desirable location, scenic surroundings, and access to amenities.

b. Consider proximity to medical facilities, shopping centers, recreational areas, and other conveniences.

c. Analyze the market potential and growth opportunities within the chosen location.

3. Concept Development and Design:

a. Collaborate with architects and design professionals experienced in senior living communities.

b. Develop a comprehensive concept that caters to independent living, assisted living, and memory care with a focus on luxury amenities.

c. Incorporate top-of-the-line amenities such as high-end dining options, spa and wellness facilities, fitness centers, recreational areas, landscaped gardens, and social spaces.

4. Regulatory and Zoning Compliance:

a. Ensure compliance with local zoning regulations and building codes.

b. Secure the necessary permits and approvals from local authorities and governing bodies.

c. Engage legal counsel and consultants to navigate any legal or regulatory complexities.

5. Financing and Business Planning:

a. Create a detailed business plan that includes financial projections, revenue models, and marketing strategies.

b. Explore financing options such as bank loans, private investors, or partnerships.

c. Prepare financial documentation and presentations to secure funding.

6. Construction and Development:

a. Hire experienced contractors, builders, and project managers to oversee construction.

b. Monitor the construction process to ensure adherence to timelines, quality control, and budgetary constraints.

c. Implement a project management system to track progress and address any issues promptly.

7. Staffing and Training:

a. Recruit and hire qualified staff, including executives, managers, caregivers, nurses, and other support personnel.

b. Develop comprehensive training programs to ensure staff members are skilled in providing high-quality care and services.

c. Emphasize customer service, empathy, and person-centered care in training modules.

8. Marketing and Branding:

a. Develop a strong brand identity and marketing strategy to attract potential residents.

b. Utilize various marketing channels such as digital marketing, social media, direct mail, and community outreach.

c. Showcase the premier amenities and luxury offerings through high-quality marketing materials, virtual tours, and engaging content.

9. Ongoing Operations and Quality Assurance:

a. Implement operational policies and procedures to maintain high standards of care and service.

b. Regularly assess and improve operations based on resident feedback and industry best practices.

c. Continuously invest in staff training, equipment upgrades, and facility maintenance to ensure the ongoing profitability and appeal of the community.

10. Resident Engagement and Retention:

a. Offer engaging activities, programs, and events to foster a sense of community and well-being.

b. Provide personalized services and amenities to meet the unique needs of residents.

c. Continuously seek feedback from residents and families to improve satisfaction and retention rates.

By following these steps, you can create a profitable, premier senior living community that offers exceptional amenities and services in a premium retirement community setting.

Chapter 20

The Two Reasons I Wrote This Book

First, I wanted to provide you with the foundational knowledge you need to intelligently approach an investment career in Senior Living.

Second, I wanted to inspire you to do it for more than just the fact that it's a safe investment. We want you to make money, but we also want you to support the aging senior population (the Silver Tsunami, as you now know it) and enjoy the difference it helps you make.

I am dedicated to your success, which is why I've written this book. I want you to have as much information as possible for your upcoming investments. So, I encourage you to read (and then re-read) this book, especially Chapter 18, as it contains what I consider to be the most important and difficult hurdle you'll find yourself confronted with, and that is understanding what type of investor you are.

The Author

Who is Vinney Chopra?

Edmund Hillary and Tenzing Norgay didn't wake up one morning in 1953 and decide to conquer Mount Everest, the world's most punishing and deadly mountain, because they had some time to kill. Their work began with routine exercises, workouts, drills, lots of preparation, and a dream; they strategized their way to the top and, in doing so, made their dream attainable for others.

The authors of this book have approached his work with a similar blend of strategy, planning, and energy, though with fewer protein bars. They understand that success, like Everest, is not a single event; the lofty goal of making people's lives better while simultaneously earning an income does not manifest without hard work, planning, and passion. Here is the team that made it happen.

Vinney "Smile" Chopra

Vinney "Smile" Chopra (MBA) is a mechanical engineer, CRE broker, author, founder of five companies, and the host of two podcasts. Chopra's nickname, "Smile," is well-earned, the result of his exuberant and high-spirited nature. He came to the US as a student with nothing but determination and the will to succeed. While his colleagues were afforded all the opportunities that come with financial stability, young Vinney had to sell encyclopedias and bibles door to door to make ends meet. His struggles finally paid off when he graduated from George Washington University with a master's degree in marketing. An ardent proponent of positive thinking and selfless actions, Vinney decided to pursue a career in the field of "relationship building and networking," honing his skills as a multifamily syndication expert. To date, Vinney has facilitated over 40 successful syndication deals. Most recently, he acquired and now manages a successful real estate investment portfolio worth over $1 billion (USD) and is currently expanding his reach, leveraging his years of expertise to create Senior Living and hospitality spaces. Vinney now oversees the management of four successful companies, all of which have flourished under his expertise: Moneil Investment Group, Moneil Management Group, Moneil Senior Living, Multifamily Syndication Academy, and Moneil Hospitality. His multifamily syndication strategies have proven successful, with a long list of satisfied residents who continue to applaud his work ethic, compassion, dedication, and positive energy. Vinney's story is truly one of rags to riches.

My Senior Living Partner, Shahid Imran

Shahid Imran is Vinney Chopra's partner in the assisted living business. To call Shahid resilient and determined would be akin to calling a supernova a "firecracker." Born in a small village with meager means but enormous drive, Shahid knew he'd need to move to the big city to realize his potential. As a young man in the workforce, Shahid noticed the subpar conditions of Senior Living residences and how these environments were not conducive to the serene, optimal living conditions he had envisioned for his own parents; he knew every senior citizen deserved better. In time, this hard-working, determined man became the owner of American Medical Equipment and worked with major insurance companies to provide for and improve upon the living conditions of senior citizens, retrofitting residences with some of the best and most durable technological equipment available.

In 2012, Shahid became increasingly dissatisfied with the conditions he witnessed within the Senior Living communities at that time and thought deeply about how to develop senior residences that were comfortable, well-designed with several amenities, but still affordable. Shahid's desire to improve the living conditions and the welfare of senior citizens drove him to sell his multi-million-dollar equipment business and start his journey toward *Build Senior Living*. Eight years later, Shahid has had an immense impact on the world of senior residences by building over 30 successful communities worth well over $500 million (USD).

Bonus

Example Senior Living Investor Brochures

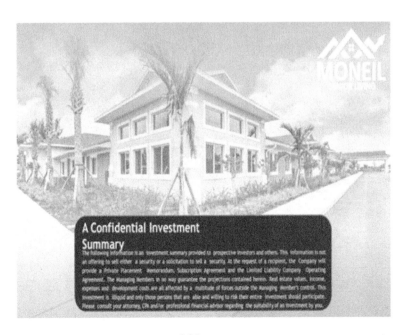

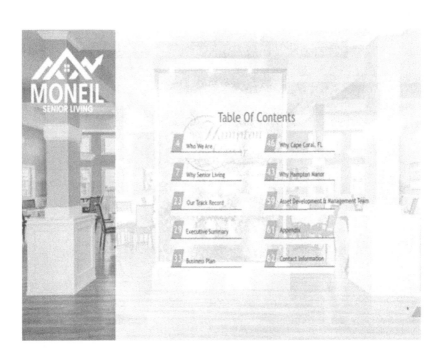

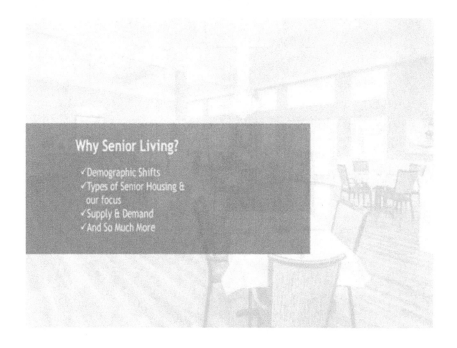

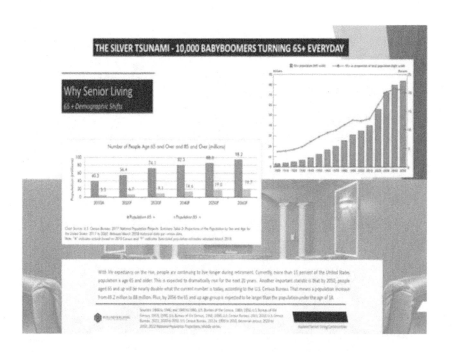

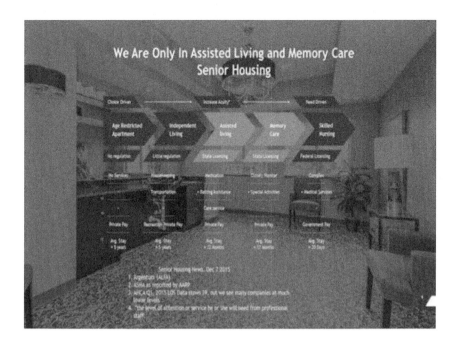

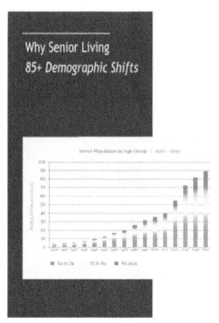

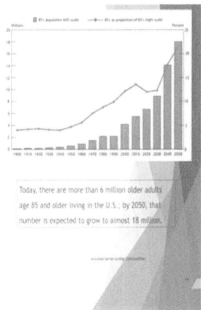

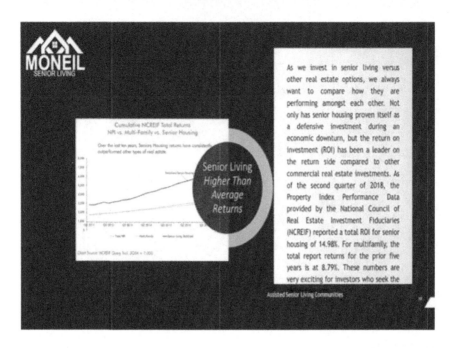

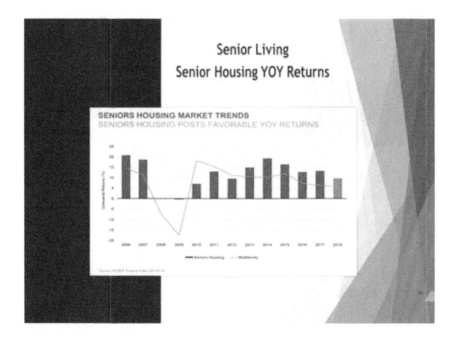

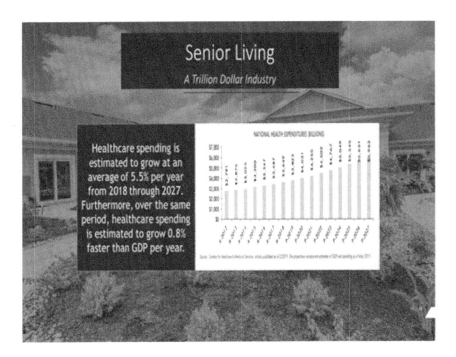

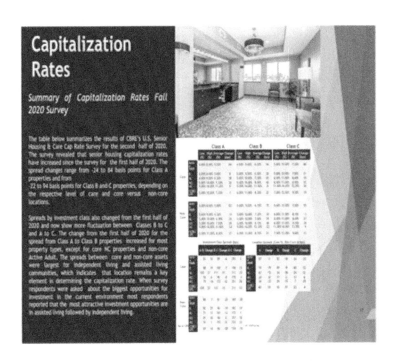

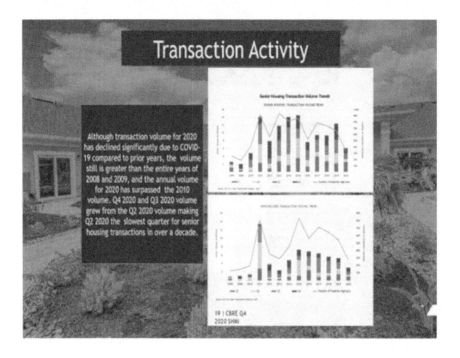

Investment **Summary**

Hampton Manor
of Cape Coral

Cape Coral, Florida

The Moneil Senior Living Team has identified Hampton Manor of Cape Coral for acquisition. This asset was built by our partner from ground zero. So we know the quality of construction is A+ with all amenities.

Please click here to take the virtual tour.

The asset consists of 88 luxury assisted living and memory care units completed and opened in June of 2020. The property offers luxury, modern, high-end finishes and amenities with universal design elements.

Situated in cape coral, a premier retirement area with strong resident demographics and operating metrics. We are purchasing for $18,000,000. During a recent appraisal it appraised for $19,500,000! Great news for our investors.

This aligns with Moneil's focus for the last 12 years in multifamily. This is an extension of our already proven model and experience. Our partner has been building these communities for the last 8 years, has built 17 of them successfully thus controlling all the development and construction inhouse

This Offering is a 506(C) and is open to accredited investors only. An Accredited investor has either a net worth of $1 million, not including their primary residence, OR an annual income of $200,00 (or $300,00 if married) for the last two years and you have a reasonable expectation that it will continue.

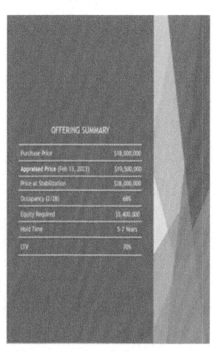

OFFERING SUMMARY

Purchase Price	$18,000,000
Appraised Price (Feb 13, 2023)	$19,500,000
Price at Stabilization	$28,000,000
Occupancy (2/28)	68%
Equity Required	$5,400,000
Hold Time	5-7 Years
LTV	70%

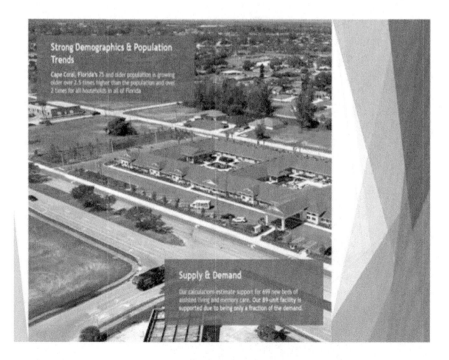

Strong Demographics & Population Trends

Cape Coral, Florida's 75 and older population is growing older over 2.5 times higher than the population and over 2 times for all households in all of Florida

Supply & Demand

Our calculations estimate support for 699 new beds of assisted living and memory care. Our 89-unit facility is supported due to being only a fraction of the demand.

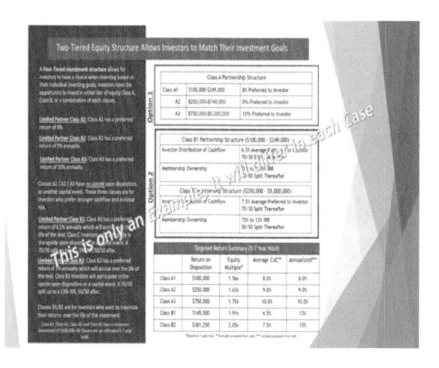

Investment Offering

The Moneil Senior Living team is pleased to present this investment offering of the 88-unit, Hampton Manor of Cape Coral assisted living and memory care community. Construction completed and the community opened in June of 2020 and is located in Cape Coral, FL. The property benefits from best-in-class amenities, concrete market fundamentals, and in a desired location for seniors retiring.

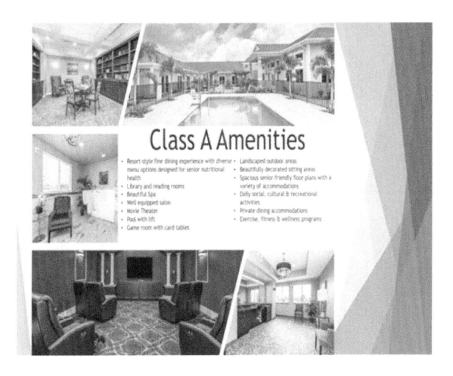

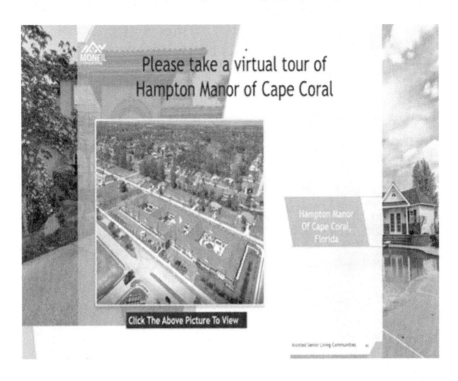

Appendix

Contact Information

Vinney
Chopra

Vinney@monilg.com

www.VinneyChopra.com

www.seniorlivinginvesting.co
www.MonetiInvest.com

BONUS CHAPTER

A Blueprint for Building an Independent and Assisted Senior Living Facility

Building an Independent and Assisted Senior Living with Memory care 94-unit facility in Punta Gorda, FL, is a complex and multi-faceted project. Below is a detailed outline of the steps, events, processes, and procedures involved:

1. Market Research and Feasibility Study:

- Conduct market research to assess the demand for senior living facilities in Punta Gorda, FL.

- Commission a feasibility study to evaluate the potential success of the project, considering demographics, competition, and financial projections.

2. Land Acquisition:

- Identify potential properties and locate a suitable 7-acre raw land parcel in Punta Gorda, FL, with access to necessary utilities and amenities.

- Negotiate with the seller to agree on a purchase price and sign a purchase agreement.

3. Due Diligence and Zoning:

- Perform due diligence to ensure the land is free from any encumbrances or legal issues.

- Check local zoning regulations and confirm that the property is zoned appropriately for the senior living facility.

- If necessary, apply for rezoning or ordinance changes to accommodate the planned facility.

4. Architectural and Design Development:

- Hire an architect and design team specializing in senior living facilities and memory care units.

- Develop detailed architectural plans and design layouts for the facility, ensuring compliance with local building codes and regulations.

5. Pre-Construction Budgeting:

- Engage a construction cost estimator to create a detailed budget for the entire project, including land acquisition, development, construction, and other associated costs.

6. Financing and Loan Procurement:

- Approach lenders or financial institutions to secure funding for the project.

- Present the project's business plan, feasibility study, and construction budget to demonstrate its viability and potential return on investment.

7. Construction Permitting:

- Obtain all necessary permits and approvals from local authorities and regulatory bodies to commence construction.

8. Construction Phase:

- Hire a reputable general contractor and subcontractors to carry out the construction.

- Monitor the construction process to ensure adherence to the approved architectural plans and timelines.

9. Hiring Personnel and Staffing:

- Recruit and hire qualified personnel for various roles in the facility, including management, nursing, caregiving, administration, maintenance, and other support staff.

10. Marketing and Pre-Leasing:

- Develop a marketing strategy to promote the senior living facility and its services to potential residents and their families.

- Start pre-leasing efforts to secure commitments from at least 70 seniors before the facility's opening.

11. Facility Furnishing and Equipment:

- Procure and install all necessary furniture, fixtures, and equipment to make the facility operational.

12. Preparing for Opening:

- Organize orientation and training programs for staff to ensure they are familiar with the facility's policies, procedures, and protocols.
- Set up administrative and operational systems, including health records management, security protocols, and resident services.

13. Grand Opening:

- Plan and execute a grand opening event to showcase the facility to the public and potential residents.
- Offer tours to interested parties and encourage new resident sign-ups.

14. Post-Opening Marketing and Operations:

- Continue marketing efforts to attract additional residents to reach full occupancy.
- Monitor and manage the facility's operations, ensuring the well-being and satisfaction of residents and compliance with all relevant regulations.

15. Ongoing Management and Maintenance:

- Establish a management team to oversee the daily operations and administration of the facility.
- Implement maintenance programs to keep the property and amenities in good condition.

An example of the cost of construction for one of our projects.

Here's an expanded example of the cost of construction for one of your senior assisted living and memory care projects (these are just numbers estimates, your project will have many factors to consider and will affect these estimates):

Let's assume you are converting a 100-suite hotel in Scottsdale, AZ, into a senior assisted living and memory care center. The cost of construction will depend on various factors, including the existing condition of the hotel, the level of renovation required, and the specific amenities and features you plan to incorporate. Please note that these figures are estimations and costs may vary depending on the local market conditions and other factors:

1. Renovation Costs:

- Suite Modifications: Renovating the suites to meet the needs of senior residents, including bathroom modifications, grab bars, wheelchair accessibility, and safety features. Estimation: $1,500 - $3,000 per suite.

- Common Areas: Upgrading common areas, including dining halls, lounges, activity rooms, and memory care units. Estimation: $100,000 - $300,000.

- Kitchen and Dining Facilities: Renovating or building a commercial-grade kitchen and dining facilities to accommodate the number of residents. Estimation: $150,000 - $300,000.

- Memory Care Unit: Creating a specialized memory care unit with additional security measures, sensory stimulation features, and safety systems. Estimation: $200,000 - $500,000.

2. Infrastructure and Utilities:

- HVAC Systems: Upgrading or replacing the heating, ventilation, and air conditioning (HVAC) systems to ensure optimal comfort for residents. Estimation: $100,000 - $200,000.

- Plumbing and Electrical: Updating plumbing and electrical systems to meet the needs of a senior care facility, including ensuring accessibility and safety compliance. Estimation: $100,000 - $200,000.

- Safety and Security: Installing fire sprinkler systems, smoke detectors, emergency lighting, surveillance cameras, and access control systems. Estimation: $50,000 - $100,000.

3. Furnishings and Equipment:

- Furniture and Fixtures: Furnishing the common areas, dining rooms, activity spaces, and memory care unit with appropriate furniture and fixtures. Estimation: $200,000 - $400,000.

- Medical Equipment: Procuring necessary medical equipment, including beds, wheelchairs, medical supplies, and monitoring systems. Estimation: $100,000 - $200,000.

- Kitchen Equipment: Purchasing commercial-grade kitchen equipment, appliances, and utensils. Estimation: $100,000 - $200,000.

4. Professional Services and Permits:

- Architectural and Design Services: Engaging architectural and design firms to develop a functional and aesthetically pleasing layout for the facility. Estimation: $50,000 - $100,000.

- Permit Fees: Covering costs associated with building permits, zoning permits, health department approvals, and other regulatory requirements. Estimation: $10,000 - $20,000.

- Legal and Consulting Fees: Seeking professional advice on legal matters, licensing, and regulatory compliance. Estimation: $10,000 - $20,000.

5. Contingency:

- Including a contingency budget to account for unforeseen expenses or changes during the construction process. Typically, a contingency of 5% to 10% of the total project cost is advisable. Estimation: $100,000 - $200,000 (assuming a 5% contingency).

Considering these estimations, the total cost of construction for converting a 100-suite hotel into a senior assisted living and memory care center in Scottsdale, AZ, could range between $1.5 million and $3 million. It's important to note that these figures are rough estimates and obtaining.

Here is an example of one of our Premier communities that we built from scratch.

GROUND-UP CONSTRUCTION: An example of the cost of construction breakdown for one of our projects. (These are just numbers estimates; your project will have many factors to consider and will affect these estimates):

COST CATEGORY	BUDGET
A Sample Project Estimate of Development	
Land	$990,000
01.01 Land Development	$300,000
01.02 Architect	$110,500
01.03 Blueprints	$20,000
01.04 Engineering	$95,000
01.05 Permits & Fees	$119,200
01.06 Surveying	$3,500
01 PRE-CONSTRUCTION	**$648,200**
02.01 Mobilization	$20,000
02 MOBILIZATION	**$20,000**
03.01 Site Clearing	$56,000
03.02 Demolition	$-
03.03 Excavation	$540,622
03.04 Sewer & Water	$65,000
03.05 Storm and Drains	$167,900
03.06 Earthwork - Other	$37,400
03 EARTHWORK & UTILITIES	**$810,922**
04.01 Footings & Foundations	$998,370
04.02 Concrete Slabs	$223,200
04.03 Sidewalks, patios & pavilions	$105,100
04.04 Concrete - Other	$61,180
04 CONCRETE	**$1,387,850**
05.01 Framing Labor	$290,990
05.04 Lumber & Building Supplies	$222,229
05.05 Rough Carpentry - Other	$37,500
05.05 Rough Carpentry - Other	$92,839
05 ROUGH CARPENTRY	**$643,558**
06.01 Roofing Labor	$72,450
06.01 Roofing Materials	$113,520
06.02 Gutters & Downspouts	
06.03 Windows	$138,770
06.04 Exterior Doors (Front Door)	
06.04 Exterior Doors	$163,449
06.05 Siding & Soffit	$41,641
06.07 Exteriors - Other	
06 EXTERIORS	**$529,830**
07.01 HVAC/Mechanical	$910,900
07 MECHANICAL	**$910,900**
08.01 Electrical	$1,123,465
08.02 Generator	$76,290
08 ELECTRICAL	**$1,199,755**

A Sample Project Estimate of Development

COST CATEGORY	BUDGET
Land	$990,000
01.01 Land Development	$300,000
01.02 Architect	$110,500
01.03 Blueprints	$20,000
01.04 Engineering	$95,000
01.05 Permits & Fees	$119,200
01.06 Surveying	$3,500
01 PRE-CONSTRUCTION	$648,200
02.01 Mobilization	$20,000
02 MOBILIZATION	$20,000
03.01 Site Clearing	$56,000
03.02 Demolition	$-
03.03 Excavation	$540,622
03.04 Sewer & Water	$65,000
03.05 Storm and Drains	$167,900
03.06 Earthwork - Other	$37,400
03 EARTHWORK & UTILITIES	$810,922
04.01 Footings & Foundations	$998,370
04.02 Concrete Slabs	$223,200
04.03 Sidewalks, patios & pavilions	$105,100
04.04 Concrete - Other	$61,180
04 CONCRETE	$1,387,850
05.01 Framing Labor	$290,990
05.04 Lumber & Building Supplies	$222,229
05.05 Rough Carpentry - Other	$37,500
05.05 Rough Carpentry - Other	$92,839
05 ROUGH CARPENTRY	$643,558
06.01 Roofing Labor	$72,450
06.01 Roofing Materials	$113,520
06.02 Gutters & Downspouts	
06.03 Windows	$138,770
06.04 Exterior Doors (Front Door)	
06.04 Exterior Doors	$163,449
06.05 Siding & Soffit	$41,641
06.07 Exteriors - Other	
06 EXTERIORS	$529,830
07.01 HVAC/Mechanical	$910,900
07 MECHANICAL	$910,900
08.01 Electrical	$1,123,465
08.02 Generator	$76,290
08 ELECTRICAL	$1,199,755

08 ELECTRICAL	**$1,199,755**
09.01 Plumbing	$1,062,406
09 PLUMBING	**$1,062,406**
10.01 Insulation	$113,679
10.02 Drywall	$808,033
10.03 Accoustical Ceilings	$47,000
10.04 Painting	$129,900
10 INTERIOR WALLS & CEILINGS	**$1,098,612**
11.01 Structural Masonry	$45,900
11.02 Non-Structural Masonry	
11.03 Stone & Brick	
11.04 Fireplaces	
11 MASONRY	**$45,900**
12.01 Finish Labor	$110,750
12.02 Interior Doors	$85,600
12.03 Trim Package	$50,000
12.04 Cabinets & Countertops	$53,472
12.04 Cabinets & Countertops	$42,301
12.04 Cabinets & Countertops	$3,500
12.04 Cabinets & Countertops	$47,600
12.05 Finish Carpentry - Other	
12 FINISH CARPENTRY	**$393,223**
13.01 Driveways & Parking Lots	$169,550
13.02 Landscaping	$159,900
13.03 Irrigation	$25,000
13.04 Fencing	$10,000
13.05 Retaining walls	
13 LANDSCAPING & GROUNDS	**$364,450**
14.01 Light Fixtures	$15,000
14.02 Flooring	$389,000
14.03 Bath Fixtures	$66,500
14.04 Wall Coverings	$15,000
14.05 Signage	$40,000
14.06 Furniture	$198,000
14.07 Room Appliances	$93,000
14.08 Allowances - Other	
14 ALLOWANCES	**$816,500**
15.01 Fire Suppression	$295,000
15.02 Commercial Kitchen	$104,000
15.03 Fire Alarm	$60,000
15.04 Nurse Call	$181,000
15.05 Security & Surveilance	$66,700

15 SPECIALS	**$706,700**
16.01 General Operating Expenses	$125,000
16.02 Equipment Rentals	$30,000
16.03 General Labor	$45,000
16.04 Temporary Utilities	$25,000
16.05 Project Closeout	$18,000
16.06 Project - Other	$35,000
16 CONSTRUCTION OPERATIONS	**$278,000**
17.01 Contingency (5%)	$661,881
17 CONTINGENCY	**$661,881**
18.01 Management Services	$400,000
18 MANAGEMENT SERVICES	**$400,000**
19.01 Professional fees/Banking	$930,800
19 Professional fees/Banking	**$930,800**
TOTAL ESTIMATED BUDGET	**$13,899,487**

This is just a sample of one of our construction project, it will vary with each site and plan!!

Final Words

I sincerely hope that you liked the content and knowledge that I tried to share in this book. You can reach me at below means:

Vinney (Smile) Chopra, MBA
Moneil Investment Group, LLC
Moneil Senior Living, LLC
Danville, CA
Vinney@Moneilig.com
www.VinneyChopra.com
www.VinneysBizCard.com
www.Moneilinvest.com
www.SeniorLivingInvesting.Co

Vinney (Smile) Chopra is a real estate investor, syndicator, International best-selling author, host of 2 Live weekly shows and a podcast, multifamily educator, mentor, dedicated husband of over 40+ years, and father of 2 children -Neil and Monica, residing in Danville, California (near San Francisco) for 40+ years. Vinney has built a portfolio of over 8500 units amounting to over $1 Billion in the multifamily, residential assisted living, and hospitality arenas. He is passionate about helping others achieve financial freedom and giving back to our seniors who have given us so much.

PS. Please check out my Amazon #1 Best Selling books:

- *Apartment Syndication Made Easy*

- *Positivity Brings Profitability*

- Check out my YouTube Channel:
  https://www.youtube.com/channel/UC_SGeOpnIHvXWqZE9dM Udlw

Book Resources Page

Grab your Free Book Bonuses at:

www.VinneyChopra.com/FreeBenefits

Or Scan This Code:

Made in the USA
Middletown, DE
10 January 2024

47578371R00139